QUILTING
FOR
BEGINNERS

QUILTING FOR BEGINNERS

Patchwork & Appliqué Projects for All Ages

by **Agnes Frank**
with instructions
by **Linda Stokes**

Drawings and diagrams by
Frank Mahood and **John Fox**

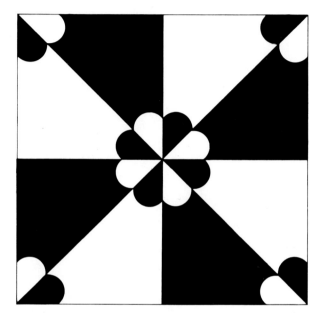

A Sterling/Main Street Book
Sterling Publishing Co., Inc.   New York

Library of Congress Cataloging in Publication Data

Franks, Agnes.
  Quilting for beginners.
  Bibliography: p. 139.
  1. Quilting. I. Stokes, Linda. II. Title.
TT835.F73 1985   746.46   85-21399

Book design by Frank Mahood
Photographs by Peter Glasser and Agnes Frank

10 9 8 7 6 5 4 3 2 1

A Sterling/Main Street Book

Published 1990 by Sterling Publishing Company, Inc.
387 Park Avenue South, New York, N.Y. 10016
© 1985 by The Main Street Press
Distributed in Canada by Sterling Publishing
% Canadian Manda Group, P.O. Box 920, Station U
Toronto, Ontario, Canada M8Z 5P9
Distributed in Great Britain and Europe by Cassell PLC
Villiers House, 41/47 Strand, London WC2N 5JE, England
Distributed in Australia by Capricorn Ltd.
P.O. Box 665, Lane Cove, NSW 2066
Printed in Hong Kong

Sterling ISBN 0-915590-72-7

Contents

Introduction: A Primer of Piecing, Appliquéing, and Quilting

QUILTING FOR BEGINNERS is simply that—a step-by-step introduction to the basics of quiltmaking through the creation of quilt blocks. Twenty different imaginative designs are presented in order of their difficulty from the basic Nine-Patch to the completely appliquéd Sunflower design. Along the way, you will be introduced to all of the useful techniques, materials, and terms of quiltmaking. A series of useful diagrams in the first chapter on the Nine-Patch design explains the steps to follow in piecing, stitching, joining rows together, quilting, and finishing. These will be referred to in succeeding chapters. In Chapter 5, devoted to the Maple Leaf design, a small bit of appliqué work is required for the first time. A special set of diagrams is provided here, too, to help you master the technique of appliqué in this project and in succeeding ones.

Starting with a quilt block is the way all quilters begin—inexperienced or not. Once such a square is completed successfully, it is easy to retrace the steps you followed and to create more blocks for a full-size quilt. But you may be just as happy with the single block itself. Several of the designs are intended to be used simply as wall hangings; others can serve as decorative squares to be applied to clothing, for use as hot pads or pillow covers, or even as baby or doll quilts. Once you have mastered the particulars of quiltmaking, you will decide what is most enjoyable and worthwhile.

But, before beginning, there are some very basic ground rules to be established. These concern selecting fabrics and colors, preparing and using fabrics, choosing supplies, making templates, and marking and cutting the fabric. These will become second nature to you. Believe me. I was a beginner once, too.

FABRIC SELECTION

Cotton—preferably 100% cotton—is the fabric best suited for quilting. It is woven firmly enough so that raveling is minimal, but it is also light enough to handle easily and sew smoothly. Cotton is soft, yet durable, and maintains a crisp, fresh appearance. Blends, however, can also be used successfully. Choose fabrics with a higher percentage of cotton than polyester —such as 65% cotton, 35% polyester. A

8

blend of this type will interact well with 100% cottons, behaving and handling more like cotton itself than polyester. Some differences will become apparent when working with blends—they tend to slip more, they are shinier, and the needle will not penetrate the fabric as easily. But blended fabrics have the advantage of wrinkling less and often have brighter, clearer colors than cotton.

Most fabric and quilting shops stock a wide variety of calicoes and solids designed especially for the quilter. But don't overlook another valuable fabric source—the scrap bag. Examine all fabrics carefully and always select the best available to ensure the best results for your efforts.

Each chapter gives a list of fabric requirements for that particular pattern. In most instances, the yardage requirements are overestimated. This will allow not only for shrinkage and error, but will also allow the large background and/or backing squares to be cut whole, rather than pieced from smaller sections.

COLOR SELECTION

Selecting a color scheme is a very individualized aspect of quilting. Two people can stitch the same traditional design, but, because of a personal sense of color, each quilter creates something quite unique. Color selection, however, can be as intimidating as it is rewarding, so a few guidelines might be helpful.

First and foremost, choose colors that are pleasing to your eye—colors that are comfortable and a joy to work with. You needn't be an expert on color theory to feel confident in selecting a successful color scheme. Observe your surroundings closely for inspiration. Your wardrobe reflects the colors you enjoy wearing and feel more

comfortable with. A favorite painting, a handsome piece of decorated china, or even a pretty dishtowel may combine colors in a particularly pleasing way. You may be inspired to re-create the charming colors of antique quilts so often photographed in country decorating magazines and quilt books. And, of course, nature provides an ever-changing and endless palette of color. Open your imagination. Experiment with different color combinations, but, above all, be happy with your selection.

Solids and prints—alone or in combination with each other—work equally well in patchwork, but their individual qualities yield different effects. Successfully combining solid fabrics together is quite easy—almost as easy as coloring with crayons. A quilt made of all solid fabrics has a sharp, bold—often modern—appearance.

Combining all printed fabrics sometimes presents a problem because of the many colors and designs involved. First, determine the color family of a printed fabric by its background color or by its overall impact when seen from a distance. Then be creative; vary the scale and type of prints used together. A light, airy print can offset a tighter, compact print to good advantage. Rosebuds don't have to be matched with other rosebuds and, in fact, often appear more stunning when teamed with vines, leaves, tiny dots, or other flowers. The point is that one print does not have to be the direct inverse of another in color or pattern in order to look well together. Variations in color and design add interest and texture to an overall color scheme. A quilt made from all printed fabrics has a soft, quaint appearance, but, when well-planned, can be as sophisticated and striking as an all solid quilt.

A logical and very natural solution to the dilemma of choosing between solids and prints is to use them together. Often, a favorite print is best emphasized with a harmonizing solid fabric. The result is a quilt with an uncomplicated, classic appearance.

While you are selecting a color scheme, keep in mind the patchwork pattern you intend to stitch. Some patterns require only two colors while others need three or four to create an interesting effect. Perhaps your pattern contains certain design elements you wish to emphasize. Light colors will allow these areas to advance, or stand out, when placed next to darker, receding colors. Remember, two different color schemes can give the same patchwork pattern two very different appearances, so think carefully about the effect you wish to achieve.

Each chapter of this book offers hints to help you choose a color scheme. Since this is a very individual matter, the final decision is yours. Look at the fabrics you have selected from a distance. Do the various colors and prints blend well together? You may need to rearrange and refine your selection several times until a pleasing and effective combination is found.

FABRIC PREPARATION

All fabrics—whether 100% cotton or cotton/polyester blends—must be washed, dried, and ironed before they are cut and sewn. Both types of fabrics shrink when laundered, but at different rates. Consequently, an article sewn from unprepared fabrics—especially one which combines cottons and blends—will pucker at the seams and possibly become distorted and ruined the first time it is laundered. Prewashing all fabrics will keep further shrinkage to a minimum and will automatically eliminate a great deal of disappointment.

Some fabrics—especially reds, dark blues, and greens—tend to bleed their colors onto lighter-colored fabrics when washed together. Test any fabric whose color-fastness is questionable. Dip a corner of the material in warm water, then squeeze the water out. If the water looks tinted, then the fabric must be washed separately until the excess dyes no longer run. If the fabric continues to bleed even after repeated washings, eliminate it from your selection.

Sort the fabrics according to lightness and darkness and launder them separately in the same manner you intend to launder the completed project. Scraps and small lengths of fabrics can become a tangled mess in the washing machine. A mesh laundry bag will hold the small pieces safely.

After the fabrics have been dried, iron them as necessary. Some fabrics will require only a light touch-up, while others will require heavier ironing. Wrinkles can be removed with a steam iron or by spraying with a fine mist of clean water from a plant mister. Any fabric which remains rumpled even after thorough ironing should be replaced. Smooth fabric is much easier to mark, cut, and sew and will enhance the overall appearance of the finished quilt.

FABRIC FACTS

Knowing a few facts concerning the weave of a fabric is very important. Along two sides of a fabric, parallel to the center fold, is an edge that looks and feels thicker than the rest of the cloth. This is known as the selvage. Its purpose is to bind the entire length of a piece of cloth to prevent raveling and distortion. The selvages, however, should always be trimmed away and never included in the seam allowances around the pattern pieces. The higher concentration of thread in the selvages will cause seams to ripple and pull.

Fabrics are folded in half lengthwise so that the two selvages meet, with the "right" side of the fabric facing outward. On the right side of the fabric, colors and prints are brighter, more obvious. On the opposite side—the "wrong" side—colors and prints seem washed out. These differences are more apparent with printed fabrics than with solid ones, so either side of a solid can be designated as the right side. It is a good idea, however, to be consistent and always use the designated side of a solid fabric as the right side just in case there are slight variations in color, texture, or sheen. The right side of a printed fabric always faces outward after stitching has been completed.

The threads of a fabric run in two directions. The threads running across the width of the cloth—or perpendicular to the selvages—indicate the crosswise grain of the fabric. The threads running the full length of the fabric—or parallel to the selvages—indicate the lengthwise grain of the fabric. The fabric will not stretch or "give" if you pull it along either the crosswise or lengthwise grains. There is considerable stretch, however, when the fabric is pulled along a diagonal line. This is known as the bias grain. The straight grain of the fabric, therefore, is along either the lengthwise or crosswise grainlines. The fabric is strong and stable on the straight grain.

Being aware of grainlines is important when marking and cutting fabric. If pattern pieces are placed carelessly on the fabric without considering the grainlines, stretched, distorted shapes that sew together poorly will certainly result. Most pattern pieces can be placed with at least one edge on the straight grain of the fabric. Arrows are printed on the pattern pieces to help the patchworker place them on the fabric correctly. Stretching will then be minimal and the shapes will sew together well.

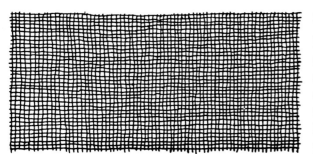
straight grain

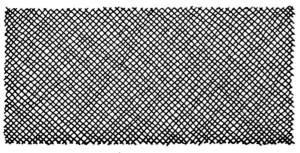
bias grain

SUPPLIES

Every quilter needs a few basic tools. Many of the items designed especially for quilters are available in fabric and quilt shops. Art supply and stationery stores are good sources for paper and measuring tools. Keep everything within easy reach so that you can work efficiently.

Paper. Lightweight tracing paper is essential for copying full-sized pattern pieces and quilting designs. However, graph paper, which is ruled in the same way as a measuring tool—first into inches, then into eighths—can be used instead. It allows you to measure and draw geometric shapes quickly and accurately.

Lightweight cardboard, index cards, and

file folders are traditional template materials, and, while they are good for this purpose, they do wear out quickly. Today, template plastic and plastic graph paper are readily available for making very precise and durable templates.

Measuring instruments. A clear plastic ruler, 18" to 24" long and 2" wide, is a valuable tool for every patchworker. Fabric and quilt shops carry a ruler of this type, often known as a "quilter's rule."

If you prefer, a metal ruler of similar proportions can be used instead of a plastic one. Avoid wooden school-type rulers and yardsticks—they tend to be inaccurate and are not always straight.

A plastic or metal right-angle triangle is necessary for measuring and marking right angles for squares, rectangles, and, of course, triangles.

The "quilter's quarter"—a clear plastic rod ¼" wide on all sides and about 6" long—is an ingenious tool used for marking quilting lines and seam allowances. It has become very popular and is widely available.

A good quality compass, purchased at an art supply store, is indispensable for drawing circles.

Scissors. Two pairs of scissors are essential. Invest in a good pair of self-sharpening dressmaker's shears, and use them for cutting fabric only. Paper and template materials should be cut with a pair of all-purpose scissors.

You might also want to have a smaller pair of scissors—such as embroidery scissors—for snipping threads and clipping seam allowances.

Keep all scissors clean and well-sharpened so they will perform smoothly and accurately.

Marking tools. A #2 lead pencil is a versatile marking tool. It can be used for drafting templates, marking the fabric, and drawing quilting lines. Pencil marks are visible on most fabrics, except perhaps the very dark ones like black and navy blue. A white dressmaker's pencil or a light-colored drawing pencil works well in this situation.

Most pencil marks can be removed during ordinary laundering. Stubborn pencil lines can be erased by spraying the fabric with a spot remover before washing. For this reason, it is always a good idea to mark lightly and test your marking tool on a scrap piece of fabric to be certain that the lines can be removed.

Never use a felt tip or ballpoint pen as a marking tool. The points on felt tips become fuzzy, and ballpoints make messy blotches. Morever, the inks used in these pens cannot be washed away.

Washable dressmaker's carbon paper, available in several colors, is helpful for reproducing quilting motifs onto the fabric. Always use a light touch when tracing over this carbon paper. *Do not* use typewriter carbon paper—it will never wash out.

Glue stick. A glue stick is available in a container that resembles a lipstick tube. It is helpful for gluing paper patterns onto cardboard and for "basting" appliqués into place. On appliqué work, however, use the stick lightly so that the fabric doesn't become stiff.

Needles. For stitching seams, a #7 or #8 Sharp needle works quite well for the beginner. Its larger size allows for easy handling.

A #7, #8, or #9 Between needle is used for quilting. It is shorter than a Sharp and allows the quilter to take smaller, finer stitches. Many seamstresses use a Between for piecing and appliqué as well as for quilting. You may also wish to switch to a Between for all your sewing after you become more accustomed to handling a needle and small pieces of fabric. Experiment until you find a comfortable size and type.

Pins. Dressmaker or silk pins are fine enough to use for piecing and pin basting. Be certain that all pins are sharp and clean.

Thimbles. A metal, plastic, or leather thimble worn on the middle finger of your sewing hand will help push and guide the needle through the fabric. Using one may seem ridiculously awkward at first, but keep trying—it really does make sewing easier and it also prevents sore fingers.

Thread. All-purpose #50 mercerized cotton or cotton-wrapped polyester thread is best. An 18″ to 20″ length of thread in your needle is sufficient.

Thread color should match the darker fabric. Using many different fabrics in one pattern, however, poses the question of what color thread is best. A neutral color—white, ivory, black, or gray—will blend into most fabric colors well enough.

For appliqué, the stitches must be as inconspicuous as possible, so match the thread color to the appliqué piece and not to the background fabric.

Thread for the final quilting of a piece is stronger and thicker than ordinary sewing thread. It is available in many colors, but the beginner should use white or ivory. This neutral color is less obvious and will help disguise the beginner's first, uncertain stitches.

Beeswax. Running the sewing and quilting threads across a piece of beeswax will enhance their strength and prevent knotting and tangling. Wrap the beeswax in a piece of cloth or wax paper to keep it fresh.

Pincushion. A pincushion and a needle case will keep pins and needles readily accessible and safe.

Quilting frames. Small, individual blocks can be quilted without the use of a frame or hoop, but a round hoop or a square will keep a larger project taut and manageable for easier quilting. A 14″ round hoop is used to quilt one area at a time on a large article. When one area has been quilted, the hoop is moved to another unquilted area. The square frame is adjustable to various sizes (usually 7″ to 14″) and is used for stretching out an entire project all at once. Choose a quilting frame to suit your needs.

MAKING TEMPLATES

The pattern pieces in patchwork are referred to as templates. Each different shape in a block requires its own template. Accuracy is extremely important. If one slight error in measuring or drawing a template occurs, the entire block will be inaccurate and the pieces will not sew together properly. Take your time. Be patient. Measure, draw, and cut a template carefully. Don't hesitate to check your work and start again if necessary.

Steps for making templates:

1. Place a sheet of tracing paper, graph paper, template plastic, or plastic graph paper over the pattern provided in the book.

2. Use your ruler and a very sharp pencil to trace the pattern. The lines you draw should be exactly on top of the lines of the master pattern.

3. Measure the shape you have drawn to

be sure its dimensions are the same as the master pattern.

4. Draw an arrow to indicate the straight grain of the fabric. Label each piece with its appropriate letter as found in the book.

5. With the paper-cutting scissors, carefully cut the pattern out directly on the lines.

If you have chosen to use template plastic or plastic graph paper, skip steps 6 and 7 because the plastic allows you to draft and cut the template all at once.

6. With the glue stick, lightly glue the paper pattern to the cardboard.

7. Cut the cardboard along the edge of the paper pattern. You now have a finished template.

8. Check the template for accuracy by measuring it or by placing it over the master pattern in the book. The edges of your template should line up exactly with the lines of the master pattern.

9. Repeat any of the above steps until an accurate template is made.

MARKING AND CUTTING THE FABRIC

Sharpen your pencils, gather your fabrics and templates, and have the list of required pieces for your pattern in plain view. Take note: only the *stitching* lines will be marked. The ¼" seam allowances needn't be marked separately, but can be estimated with a ruler or the quilter's quarter.

Steps for marking and cutting the fabric:

1. Unfold the fabric so that it is only one layer thick. Place it on a hard, flat surface (such as a table top), and smooth out any ripples.

2. Trim away the selvages.

3. The *wrong* side of the fabric must face toward you. All markings for patchwork are made on the wrong side of the fabric.

4. Place the template straight on the fabric, about ¼" away from the edges. Use a ruler or the quilter's quarter to help gauge this measurement. Position the template so that the arrow is going in the same direction as the lengthwise (or crosswise) grain of the fabric. Hold the template firmly.

5. With a very sharp pencil, draw around all the edges of the template, making sure to mark the corners accurately. Angle the pencil in toward the template so that the line drawn will be as close as possible to the template's edge. Press firmly enough to make a visible line, but not so firmly that the pencil pulls and stretches the fabric as you mark. A light, quick stroke of the pencil, similar to striking a match, will make a fine line.

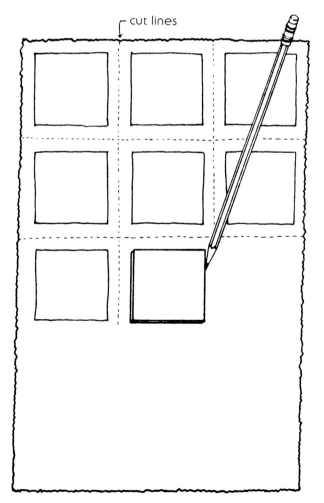

cut lines

14

6. Move the template about ½″ away from the shape just drawn. Use a ruler or two widths of the quilter's quarter to help judge this distance until you become confident estimating it. This space will provide the ¼″ seam allowances for two adjacent shapes. It is better to have the seam allowances slightly larger than ¼″ rather than smaller. Any excess can be trimmed away later. Draw around the template again. Repeat steps 5 and 6 until the required number of patches has been marked.

7. With the fabric shears, cut the shapes apart. *Do not cut on the lines you have drawn.* Remember, these are the stitching lines. Cut *evenly* between the lines so that each shape will have an extra ¼″ of fabric on all sides. This is the seam allowance.

Making templates for large pattern pieces, background blocks, backing squares, batting, and binding strips is optional. Instead, they can be measured and drawn directly onto the fabric with a ruler and a right-angle triangle. (The measurements provided for large pattern pieces are the finished dimensions, so be certain to add the ¼″ seam allowances. Except where noted, the measurements provided for the backing squares, background blocks, batting, and binding strips *include* seam allowances.) Work with the straight grain of the fabric for all these pieces. If you feel more comfortable making a template, by all means, do so.

PIECING ORDER

Each chapter gives detailed instructions for the easiest and most logical way to piece that particular patchwork pattern. It is always helpful to refer to the diagrams for the correct color and stitching order.

PRESSING

Pressing the completed patchwork block will not only help it to lie flat, but it will also give it a more polished appearance. From the wrong side, press the seam allowances *together* in one direction, away from the lighter fabric whenever possible. Take care not to stretch the fabric as you press. Iron the right side of the patchwork to remove any wrinkles.

SANDWICHING AND BASTING

A quilt would certainly not be a quilt without its three layers of fabric.

The backing fabric can be plain, unbleached muslin, or, for added interest, a print or solid-color fabric which coordinates with the patchwork top. The backing fabric is always cut about 1″ larger all around than the finished size of the patchwork top.

The batting gives a quilt its characteristic fluffiness and warmth. Beginners should use only bonded polyester batting because it is easy to handle and requires less quilting than cotton or wool batting. Polyester batting is available in several thicknesses. Choose a traditional quilt batt thickness, not a comforter thickness. The batting is also cut about 1″ larger all around than the finished size of the patchwork top.

And finally, the patchwork top completes the "sandwich."

To assemble the layers, place the backing fabric, wrong side up, on a flat surface. Smooth out any wrinkles. Then, carefully place the batting on top of the backing, again smoothing out any wrinkles but taking care not to stretch it. Center the patchwork top (right side up) over the two previous layers, and place a few pins through all three layers.

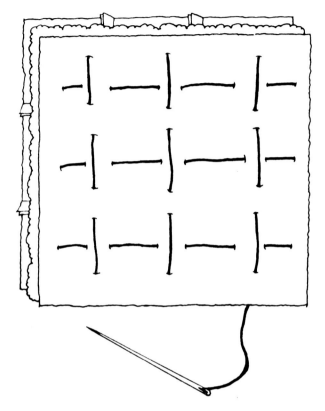

Baste the layers together with long running stitches, beginning at the center and working outwards. Make several horizontal and vertical rows of basting stitches about 3" to 4" apart across the entire surface of the sandwich. Remove the pins when the basting has been completed.

QUILTING

The three layers are held permanently in place with small quilting stitches. There really is no mystery to the quilting stitch— it very closely resembles an ordinary running stitch. The only difficulty lies in penetrating the thickness of three layers of fabric while still being able to achieve fine,

even stitches. With practice and patience, your quilting skills will gradually improve. Don't be overly critical or ashamed of your first stitches. Just keep trying.

Most of the patterns in the following chapters use either outline or other straight-line quilting designs. Refer to the individual quilting diagrams for assistance in reproducing the necessary quilting lines. Outline quilting emphasizes the patchwork design by following the seam lines of certain patches. In this instance, measure ¼" away from the appropriate seam lines with a ruler or a quilter's quarter; draw a fine, light line with a #2 pencil or a dressmaker's pencil at this distance. Occasionally, outline quilting is done ⅛" (or less) away from the seam lines, so marking is not necessary. Simply follow the edges of the patches as closely and evenly as possible.

Other straight quilting lines create a pattern which does not follow the seams of the patchwork. Instead, they form an entirely different design of their own. Again, refer to the individual quilting diagram, and draw the appropriate lines with a ruler and pencil.

The beginner will also have the opportunity to try quilting gently curved lines that outline curved patches as well as some simple flower motifs such as the tulip (Chapter 19) and the sunflower (Chapter 20).

Detailed instructions and diagrams of the actual quilting method are presented in Chapter 1.

FINISHING

The edges of a quilted article must be bound to give it a finished appearance. Binding strips, two layers thick, in a matching or contrasting fabric, are stitched to each side of the quilted sandwich for a durable edge. Once this is done, stand back and admire your finished project.

Detailed instructions for cutting and stitching the bindings are given in Chapter 1.

QUILTING FOR BEGINNERS

1. Nine-Patch: Starting with the Basic Square

THE NINE-PATCH block is simply designed and easily pieced, making it an ideal pattern for the beginner's first lesson in patchwork. Many of the basic techniques of all patchwork can be learned successfully while working with this simple pattern. The name "Nine-Patch" describes how the block is constructed. Nine squares—or patches—are arranged into three rows of three squares each. Only one pattern piece or template—a 4" square—is needed to construct the entire block.

Notice that an overall design is formed by alternating light and dark patches of fabric. A dark cross seems to appear when four dark squares are set together with five lighter or contrasting squares. For example: if the dark patches are represented by red, either white or a lighter shade of red for the remaining patches will provide enough contrast to bring out the cross design.

Choose two fabrics whose colors combine well with each other in a color scheme pleasing to your eye. For a first project it is especially important to choose colors you will enjoy looking at and working with. Remember also that contrast between light and dark is the basic idea behind the Nine-Patch. If in doubt about your selection, look at the fabrics from a distance. Do you see a good amount of contrast? Continue to experiment with different combinations until a pleasing arrangement is found.

TOOLS

Assemble all the template-making and sewing supplies listed on pgs. 10-12.

FABRIC REQUIREMENTS

For a 12" (completed size) Nine-Patch block, you will need:

1. ¼ yard of 45"-wide pre-washed cotton fabric for dark patches (color #1);

2. ¼ yard of 45"-wide pre-washed cotton fabric for contrasting patches (color #2);

3. ½ yard of pre-washed unbleached muslin or other cotton fabric for backing;

4. Polyester batting;

5. An additional ¼ yard of 45"-wide pre-washed cotton fabric for binding, color #1 or #2.

TEMPLATES

Following the general instructions for making templates described on pgs. 12-13, draw and cut one template from the full-sized pattern piece A. Be certain to check your template for accuracy.

MARKING AND CUTTING THE FABRIC

Refer to the general instructions outlined on pgs. 13-14. A 2″-wide ruler (18″ to 24″ long) can serve as a template for measuring and marking all binding strips. Lay the ruler along the straight grain of the fabric, measure the required lengths and number of strips, and mark around all edges of the ruler with a pencil. *Do not* add the usual ¼″ seam allowances. Cut the strips apart. With the quilter's quarter, mark the ¼″ seam line along one long edge of the right side of each binding strip.

The Nine-Patch block will require:

1. 4 A pieces in dark fabric (color #1);

2. 5 A pieces of contrasting fabric (color #2);

3. 2 binding strips 13½″ long by 2″ wide, either color #1 or #2;

4. 2 binding strips 14½″ long by 2″ wide, either color #1 or #2;

5. 13½″ square for backing;

6. 13½″ square of batting.

straight grain

A

Full-sized pattern piece. Add ¼″ seam allowance.

PIECING ORDER

Arrange the cut A pieces into three rows of three squares each according to the piecing diagram. Refer frequently to this diagram while pinning and stitching to be certain you are following the correct color sequence.

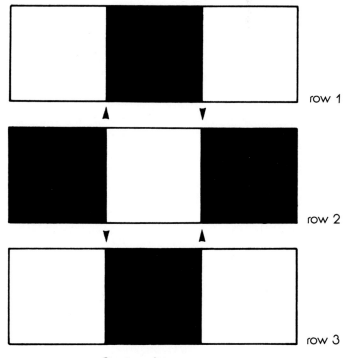

row 1

row 2

row 3

Piecing diagram

PINNING

1. Place a dark square, color #1, and a contrasting square, color #2, together with the right sides facing each other. The wrong side with the marked stitching lines will be facing out toward you (see fig. a).

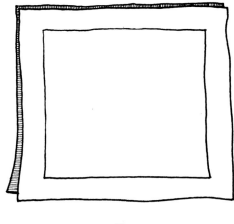

Fig. a

2. Put a pin in the right-hand corner of the top square. Turn the fabric over so you can see the bottom square. Pierce the corresponding corner of the bottom square with the pin point. Let the pin hang loose rather than bringing it back through to the front. Repeat with the left-hand corner (see fig. b).

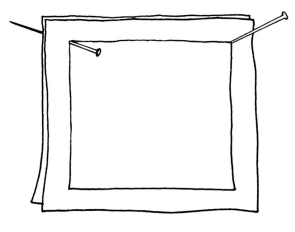

Fig. b

3. Place a third pin on the seam line halfway between the corners. Turn the patches over again to be certain that the pin has gone through the stitching line on the bottom square. If not, remove the pin and gently slide the fabric up or down until the pin does go through both stitching lines. Bring all the pins forward to the front to secure (see fig. c).

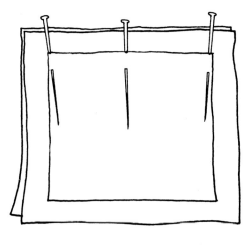

Fig. c

STITCHING

1. Hold the two pinned squares in your non-sewing hand.

2. From the back, insert the threaded needle into the fabric at the right-hand corner, exactly in the same spot as the pin (see fig. d). Remove the pin. Take one small stitch

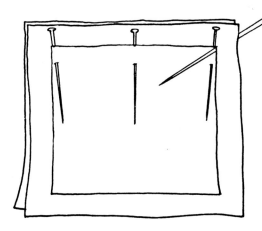

Fig. d

forward (fig. e) and then one small

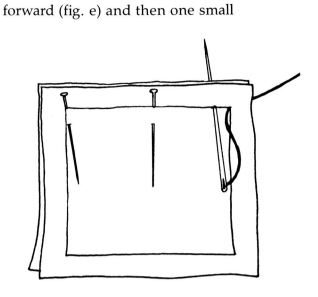

Fig. e

Fig. g

backstitch (figs. f, g, and h). A backstitch is simply a repeat of a stitch already taken.

Fig. f

Fig. h

3. Take small running stitches right on the marked seam line, removing the pins as you come to them (figs. i and j). Turn the

4. End the stitching exactly where the left-hand corner has been pinned. Remove the pin and take a small backstitch (fig. k).

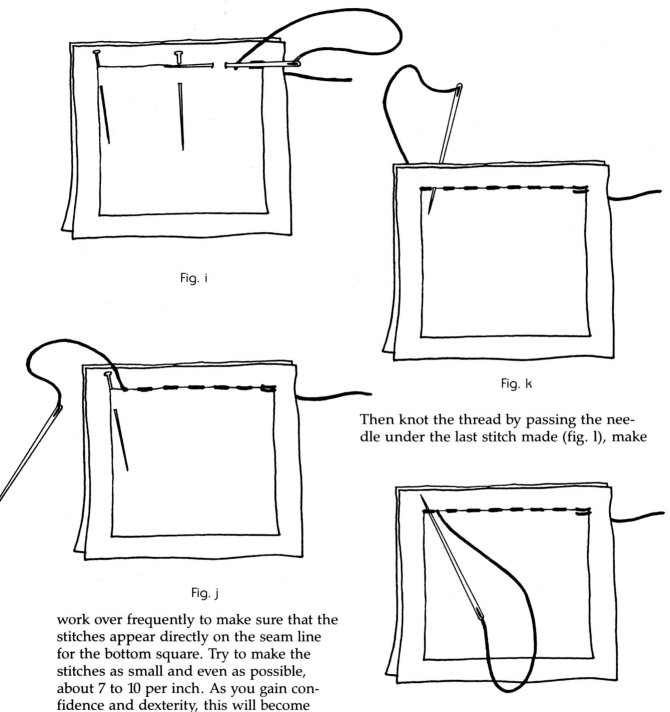

Fig. i

Fig. k

Fig. j

Then knot the thread by passing the needle under the last stitch made (fig. l), make

work over frequently to make sure that the stitches appear directly on the seam line for the bottom square. Try to make the stitches as small and even as possible, about 7 to 10 per inch. As you gain confidence and dexterity, this will become easier.

Fig. l

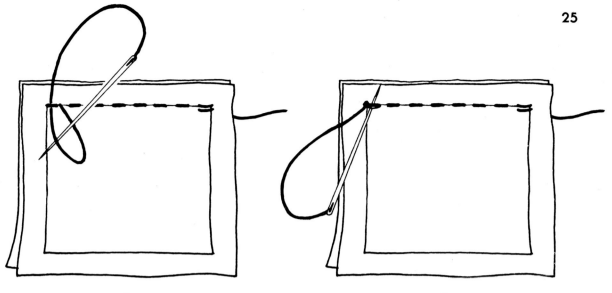

Fig. m

Fig. n

a thread loop, pass the needle through the loop (fig. m), and pull snugly. Make a second knot in the same way (fig. n). Clip the thread close to the knot.

5. Trim any seam allowances that are uneven or larger than ¼".

6. Continue pinning and stitching the squares together in this manner until three separate rows have been completed. Remember to follow the proper color sequence shown in the piecing diagram.

JOINING THE ROWS TOGETHER

1. Place row 1 and row 2 together with the right sides facing each other (see fig. o).

Once again, the wrong side of the fabric with the marked seam lines will be facing you.

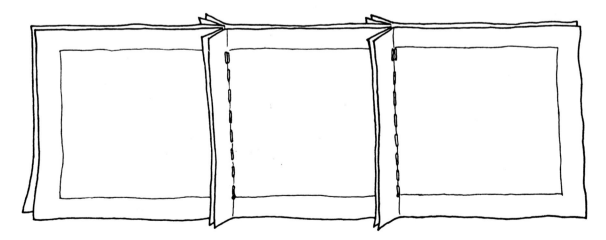

Fig. o

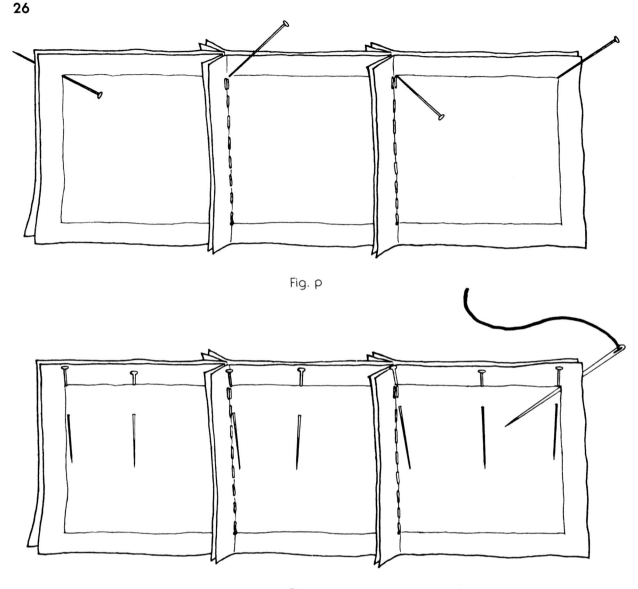

Fig. p

Fig. q

2. Pin the right- and left-hand corners of the two rows together in the same way as you matched corners before. Turn the seam allowances to the left, pressing them firmly between thumb and forefinger to make them lie flat (see fig. p).

3. Place a pin in the left-hand corner of the first square on the top row (see fig. p again). Push it through to the corresponding corner of the square on the bottom row. Make certain that the corners match precisely. Do not pin the seam allowances down.

4. Repeat step 3 with the remaining set of squares on the row.

5. Add more pins along the seam line, matching both sets of seam lines exactly. Bring all the pins forward to secure. Beginning at the right-hand corner, stitch as before (see fig. q).

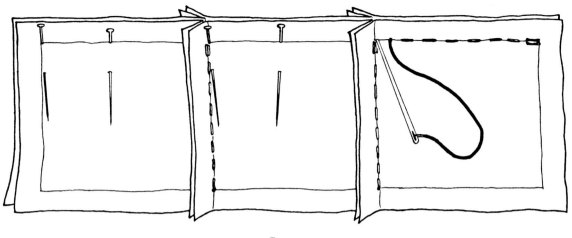

Fig. r

6. When you reach the first intersection, put the needle precisely through the left-hand corner of the top square and remove the pin (see fig. r). Push the needle through to the corresponding corner of the square underneath.

7. Take a backstitch right over the stitch just

made in step 6. (Fig. s shows this stitch beginning to be made.)

8. The needle and thread are now on the bottom row, so turn your work over to see it better. Slide the needle through the seam allowances of the first two squares on the bottom row (see fig. t). Do not sew down the seam allowances (see fig. u).

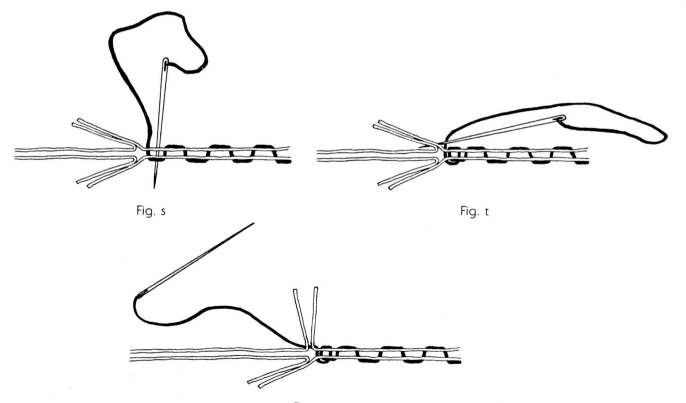

Fig. s

Fig. t

Fig. u

9. Now, turn the seam allowances to the right. From the back, push the needle through the right-hand corner of the sec- ond square on the row to the corresponding corner of the second square on the top row (see fig. v).

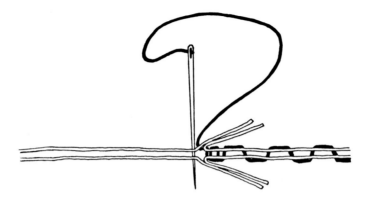

Fig. v

10. Take a small stitch forward (see fig. w) and then a backstitch.

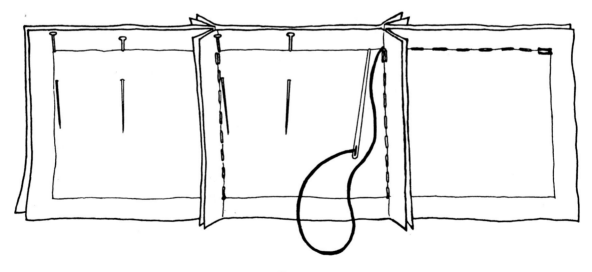

Fig. w

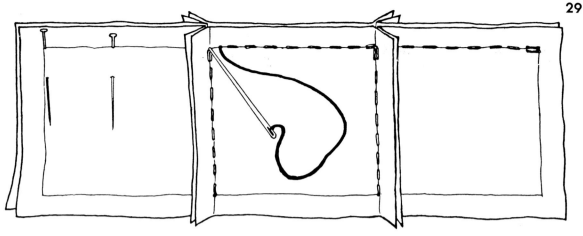

Fig. x

11. Continue stitching the rows together and matching the intersections in this way. End at the very last corner on the row and knot as before (see fig. x).

12. Open your work to the right side. Check to see that all the intersections match precisely.

13. Attach row 3, using the same method described above.

14. When the entire block has been completed, press the seam allowances and the top side as described on pg. 14.

QUILTING

Preparing to quilt. The Nine-Patch is quilted very simply with straight lines that form an "X" through each square (see quilting diagram). Because of its small size, the Nine-Patch block can be quilted without a hoop or frame. Simply roll up one side of the block and hold it in your non-sewing hand so that the forefinger of this hand can be directly under the spot to be quilted.

1. With a ruler and a #2 pencil or a dressmaker's pencil, mark two diagonal lines, from corner to corner, in each square.

2. Sandwich the three layers of fabric together as described on pg. 14. First, the

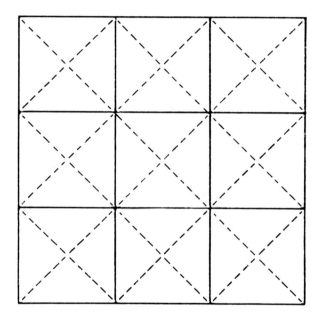

Quilting diagram

13½" square of backing fabric; second, the 13½" square of batting; third, the pressed and marked patchwork top. Pin. Then baste through all three layers.

3. Thread a #7 or #8 Between needle with a single strand of either white or ivory quilting thread about 18" to 20" long; knot one end. Run the thread across beeswax twice; then remove the excess by running the thread between your thumb and forefinger.

As a general rule, quilting should begin in the center and work toward the edges so that any extra fullness or wrinkles can be smoothed outwards. Begin at the very center square of the Nine-Patch.

Burying the knot. This is an essential first step.

1. From the *top*, insert the needle into the fabric about ½" away from the corner of the center square patch. *Do not* go through all three layers to the back.

2. Pass the needle sideways under the patchwork and through the batting.

3. Bring the needle back to the top at the exact spot you wish to begin, pulling the thread so the knot meets the patchwork top (see fig. y).

4. Gently tug on the thread so that the knot pops through the fabric and remains buried in the batting.

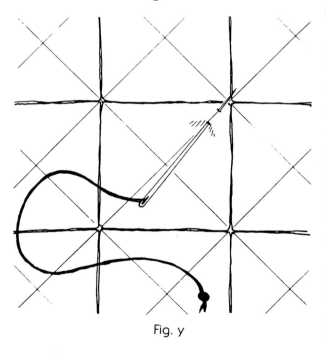

Fig. y

Quilting stitch. The first quilting stitch will be taken right in front of the thread coming out of the patchwork top.

1. Insert the needle into the fabric again a very short distance away. This time, penetrate all three layers until you feel the point touch the forefinger of the non-sewing hand underneath. Be careful not to prick your finger!

2. Pull the thread through the layers with enough tension to create a "dimpled" look on the patchwork top.

3. Continue stitching in this manner, directly on top of the marked lines. Eventually you will be able to stack two or three quilting stitches on the needle at one time before pulling the thread all the way through.

As described earlier with the running stitches used in piecing the block, the quilting stitches will not be perfect at first. Try to keep them as straight and as equal in length as possible. Again, 5 to 6 per inch is a reasonable goal; eventually, you should be able to stitch 7 to 10 per inch.

Ending. When you finish a complete line of quilting (or run out of thread), you must bury another knot in the batting to keep the quilting secure.

1. Make a loop knot in the thread about ¼" away from where the thread last came out of the patchwork.

2. Then, pretend you are taking another quilting stitch, only this time do not go through all three layers but pass the needle under the patchwork and through the batting, and then back up to the top.

3. Pull the thread until the knot pops through the fabric and remains buried in the batting.

4. Clip the thread close to the patchwork top.

Quilt all the marked lines following the steps outlined.

FINISHING

1. Remove all the basting stitches.

2. Carefully trim the excess batting and backing evenly with the patchwork top.

3. Fold each binding strip in half lengthwise, *wrong sides* together. Press.

4. With *right sides* together and all raw edges even, pin the two 13½" long binding strips to two parallel edges on the quilted block. Make certain that the seam lines match. The binding strips will be slightly longer than these edges. Distribute the extra length evenly at each side. Starting at the right, stitch along the seam line through all thicknesses using a #7 or #8 Sharp needle and a double strand of thread. To reduce bulk, trim the seam to a scant ¼" width. Then trim the excess binding on each end so that it is even with the edge of the quilted block.

5. Fold the binding over the seam towards the backing, and finger press. Place the folded edge of the binding just over the stitched seam line so that it hides these stitches. Pin into place.

6. Thread the needle with a color thread to match the binding. Stitch the folded edge of the binding to the backing, using small, almost invisible stitches (see appliqué stitching diagram, p. 50). These stitches should pierce just the very edge of the folded binding, but must also pick up about ⅟₁₆" of backing fabric *underneath* the binding.

7. Repeat steps 3 and 4 with the 14½"-long binding strips on the remaining edges. *Do not* trim the excess binding this time. Fold each end in so that it is even with the edge of the binding perpendicular to it. Do not allow any ends to peek out.

Continue with steps 5 and 6.

8. Stand back and admire all the work you have done to accomplish your first quilted project!

2. Pinwheel: A Variation on the Square

THE PINWHEEL variation of the Four-Patch block is another simple pattern for the beginner, but one which takes patchwork a step further than the Nine-Patch. Two smaller units—in this instance, triangles—are pieced together to form one larger unit, a square. Then, the four square patches (hence, the name "Four-Patch") are stitched together to form one large square for the completed pattern. Many of the more complicated patchwork patterns are constructed in a similar way from smaller units into larger ones which eventually form the completed design. Mastering the technique for piecing the Pinwheel block will help the beginner learn the skills necessary for piecing more intricate patchwork patterns. A self-finishing method, instead of the usual binding method, will also be introduced.

The Pinwheel pattern is the namesake of the toy that has delighted children for many generations. Remember how the bright colors blurred together as the pinwheel turned around and around? For your Pinwheel block, you may wish to choose a brilliant color scheme that reminds you of your favorite pinwheel. Or you may wish to choose a softer combination, perhaps two pretty pastel shades. While experimenting with different colors and prints, remember that a good amount of contrast between two fabrics is needed to enhance the Pinwheel effect.

TOOLS

Assemble all the template-making and sewing supplies listed on pgs. 10-12.

FABRIC REQUIREMENTS

For an 8" (completed size) Pinwheel block, you will need:

1. ¼ yard of 45"-wide pre-washed cotton fabric for dark patches (color #1);

2. ¼ yard of 45"-wide pre-washed cotton fabric for contrasting patches (color #2);

3. ⅜ yard of pre-washed unbleached muslin or other cotton fabric for backing;

4. Polyester batting.

TEMPLATES

Refer to the general instructions on pgs. 12-13 for making templates. Use the full-sized pattern piece to make one template.

MARKING AND CUTTING THE FABRIC

Refer to the general instructions on pgs. 13-14 for marking and cutting the fabric. The Pinwheel block will require:

1. 4 A pieces from dark fabric (color #1);

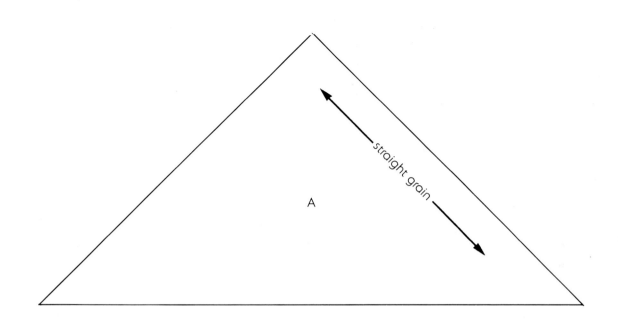

A

straight grain

Full-sized pattern piece. Add ¼" seam allowance.

2. 4 A pieces from contrasting fabric (color #2);

3. One 8½" square from backing fabric. This piece needs no template. Simply measure and mark the square onto the fabric using your ruler and right-angle triangle.

4. One 8½" square of batting.

PIECING ORDER

Match one piece of each color to form a square unit for a total of four units. Two rows of two units each will complete the pattern. To ensure the correct color sequence, refer to the piecing diagrams a and b while stitching.

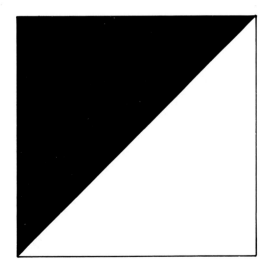

Piecing diagram a

PINNING AND STITCHING

1. Using the same pinning method described for the Nine-Patch, pin one A piece of color #1 to a second A piece of color #2 along the longest edge of the triangle (see piecing diagram a).

2. Stitch the two A pieces together along the marked seam line, using the same technique as for the Nine-Patch.

3. Repeat steps 1 and 2 with the remaining A pieces until you have four completed squares.

4. Refer to piecing diagram b and arrange the square units into two rows of two squares each.

5. Pin and stitch the square units of row 1 together, making certain to match the cor-

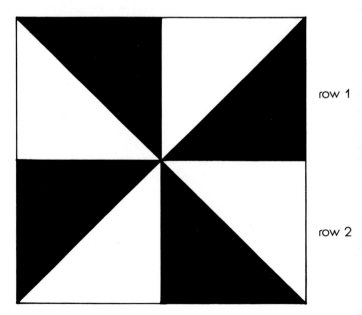

row 1

row 2

Piecing diagram b

ners exactly and to keep the seam allowances free.

6. Repeat step 5 for row 2.

7. Pin rows 1 and 2 together, using the same method for pinning the rows of the Nine-Patch together. Getting all the seam lines to match exactly in the center of the block presents a challenge, so pin the corners carefully.

8. Stitch the two rows together using the same method learned for the Nine-Patch.

9. Press the seam allowances and the top side of the completed Pinwheel block as described on pg. 14.

FINISHING

1. Place the patchwork top, right side up, on top of the batting. Baste together.

2. Place the backing fabric on top of the patchwork/batting sandwich, *right sides together.* The three layers will be in this order: batting, Pinwheel block, backing. This is not the usual order for sandwiching the layers, but it will enable you to turn the entire piece so that all the raw edges will be inside and a self-finished edge will be on the outside. Pin the edges together, matching the corners as before.

3. Stitch on the seam line around the entire block, but leave a small opening, about 1½″ long in the middle of one side. Be certain to stitch through all three layers. Trim the seam allowances if necessary.

4. Turn the block right side out through the small opening. Now the layers should be in the usual order: backing (right side facing outward), batting (hidden inside), and the Pinwheel block (right side facing outward). Turn the seam allowances of the little opening inward and stitch closed with small, hidden stitches.

QUILTING

1. Refer to the general quilting directions on pg. 15. Mark the quilting lines (see quilting diagram) on the patchwork top.

2. Quilt along the marked lines.

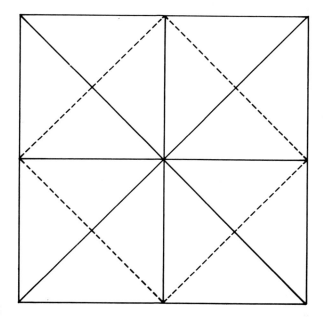

Quilting diagram

3. Checkerboard: Combining the Squares

THE CHECKERBOARD pattern is actually an elongated version of the Nine-Patch. All the same techniques, from start to finish, are repeated in the Checkerboard pattern to help reinforce and refine the skills you have acquired so far.

For all its simplicity in design, the Checkerboard pattern is certainly capable of creating a very strong—but appealing—visual impact. Color selection should again emphasize the contrast between two colors so that the checkerboard effect is obvious. You may want to try the traditional black and red color scheme, but many other color combinations will work just as well.

TOOLS

Assemble all the template-making and sewing supplies listed on pgs. 10-12.

FABRIC REQUIREMENTS

A 14″ (completed size) Checkerboard block will require:

1. ¼ yard of 45″-wide pre-washed cotton fabric for color #1;

2. ¼ yard of 45″-wide pre-washed cotton fabric for color #2;

3. ¼ yard of 45″-wide pre-washed cotton fabric in color #3 for the binding;

4. ½ yard of 45″-wide unbleached muslin or other cotton fabric for the backing;

5. Polyester batting.

TEMPLATES

Refer to the general instructions for making

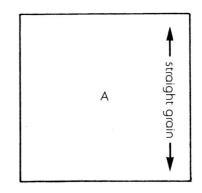

Full-sized pattern piece. Add ¼″ seam allowance.

templates outlined on pgs. 12-13. Use the full-sized pattern piece to draw and cut two or three templates. Remember, cardboard templates fray quite easily after numerous markings, and thus become inaccurate. Use the extra templates as replacements whenever necessary.

MARKING AND CUTTING THE FABRIC

Mark and cut the fabric as before, referring to the general instructions on pgs. 13-14. The Checkerboard pattern requires:

1. 32 A pieces from color #1;

2. 32 A pieces from color #2;

3. 2 strips 15½" long by 2" wide from color #3 for binding;

4. 2 strips 16½" long by 2" wide from color #3 for binding;

5. 15½" square for backing;

6. 15½" square of batting.

PIECING ORDER

Refer to the color sequence shown in piecing diagram a and arrange 4 A pieces of each color into a row. Arrange the remaining A pieces into additional rows as needed.

row 1

Piecing diagram a

PINNING AND STITCHING

1. Starting on one end of the row (see piecing diagram a), pin and stitch one A piece of color #1 to one A piece of color #2, using the same pinning and stitching methods as before. Continue pinning and stitching ad-

ditional A pieces together until the entire row is completed.

2. Piece 7 more rows in the same manner, referring to the piecing diagram when necessary to keep the correct color sequence.

3. To join the rows together, refer to piecing diagram b. The checkerboard effect is achieved by simply turning the strip for row 2 so that the color placement is opposite to that of row 1. Pin and stitch the two rows together in the same manner as for the Nine-Patch.

4. Repeat step 3 with the remaining six rows until the entire Checkerboard block has been completed (see piecing diagram c).

5. Press the seam allowances and the top of the patchwork block as before.

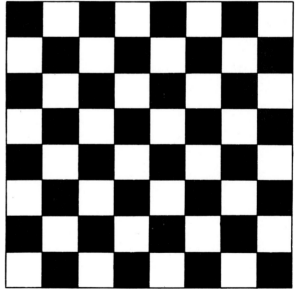

Piecing diagram c

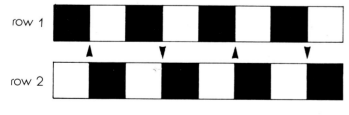

row 1

row 2

Piecing diagram b

QUILTING

1. Refer to the general quilting instructions on pg. 15. To guide you in marking the quilting lines on the top side of the Checkerboard block, see quilting diagram.

2. Sandwich and baste the backing, batting, and patchwork top together just as before.

3. Quilt along the marked lines.

FINISHING

1. Remove the basting stitches.

2. Trim the excess batting and backing evenly with the quilted top.

3. Pin and stitch the two 15½"-long binding strips to parallel edges on the Checkboard block. Refer to pg. 31 for finishing advice.

4. Repeat step 3 with the two 16½"-long binding strips on the remaining edges.

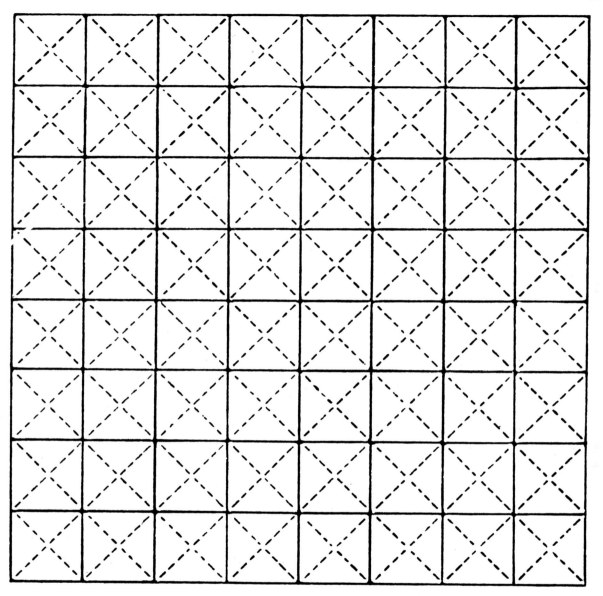

Quilting diagram

4. Churn Dash: Adding Triangles to Squares

MANY OF THE PATCHWORK patterns handed down from generation to generation were designed and named by homemakers who drew their inspiration from everyday household objects. One such pattern is the Churn Dash, which is said to represent the dasher on an old-fashioned butter churn. Perhaps the dream of a quilt in this pattern kept the homemaker's imagination occupied while she engaged in the time-consuming and monotonous task of churning butter.

At first glance, the Churn Dash pattern appears more difficult than it really is. Even though you will be working with two pattern pieces and three colors, all the construction techniques are the same as those used before.

By now you have learned to recognize the main design element of a particular patchwork pattern and how to emphasize it through the use of color and contrast. For the Churn Dash pattern, select two coordinating fabrics for the "dasher" patches and a third fabric for the background patches.

TOOLS

Assemble all the template-making and sewing supplies listed on pgs. 10-12.

FABRIC REQUIREMENTS

For a 12″ (completed size) Churn Dash block you will need:

1. ¼ yard of 45″-wide pre-washed cotton fabric for color #1;

2. ¼ yard of 45″-wide pre-washed cotton fabric for color #2;

3. ¼ yard of 45″-wide pre-washed cotton fabric for color #3;

4. ¼ yard of 45″-wide pre-washed cotton fabric for binding strips, any of the above colors;

5. ½ yard of 45″-wide pre-washed cotton fabric for backing;

6. Polyester batting.

TEMPLATES

Make one template each for the full-sized pattern pieces A and B. If necessary, refer again to the general instructions for making templates on pgs. 12-13.

MARKING AND CUTTING THE FABRIC

Mark and cut the fabric according to the method described on pgs. 13-14. The Churn Dash block requires:

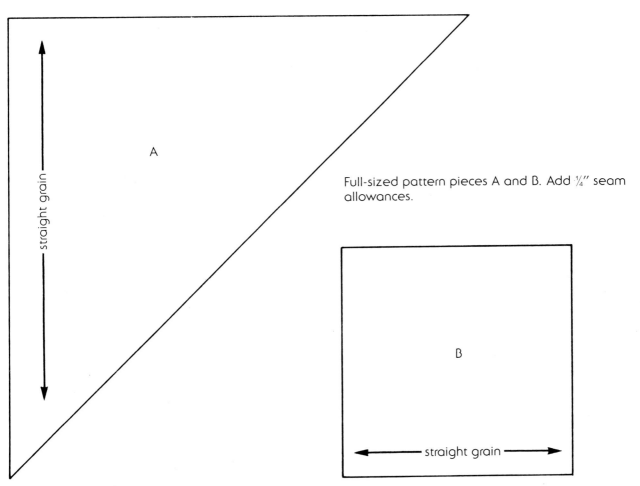

Full-sized pattern pieces A and B. Add ¼″ seam allowances.

1. 4 A pieces from color #1;

2. 4 A pieces from color #3;

3. 4 B pieces from color #2;

4. 5 B pieces from color #3;

5. Two 13½″-long by 2″-wide binding strips and

6. Two 14½″-long by 2″-wide binding strips, all from the same fabric;

7. 13½″ square for backing;

8. 13½″ square of batting.

PIECING ORDER

The Churn Dash block is constructed from

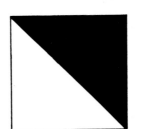

Piecing diagram a

two basic units (see piecing diagram a): a square made from two A pieces and a rectangle made from two B pieces. Then, these units are joined into rows (see piecing diagram b). Arrange the A pieces from color #1 with the A pieces from color #3. Match the B pieces of color #3 to the B pieces of color #2. You will have one B piece from color #3 without a mate.

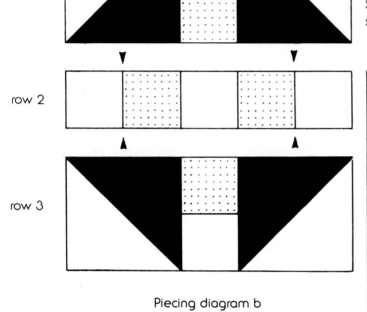

row 1

row 2

row 3

Piecing diagram b

PINNING AND STITCHING

Refer to piecing diagrams a and b while pinning and stitching to be certain you are placing the patches in the correct order. Use the now familiar method first described for the Nine-Patch on pgs. 22-25 to pin and stitch the patches together.

1. Make four square units, each from two A pieces in colors #1 and #3.

2. Make four rectangular units, each from two B pieces in colors #2 and #3.

3. Pin and stitch the smaller units into rows

as shown in diagram b. Notice that rows 1 and 3 are constructed from the same units, but that the darker triangles are in different positions. Take care to place these units correctly. Row 2 is constructed from two rectangular units with the extra B piece in color #3 added to the end of the strip.

4. Pin and stitch the rows together to form the completed Churn Dash block (see piecing diagram c).

5. Press the seam allowances and the right side of the block.

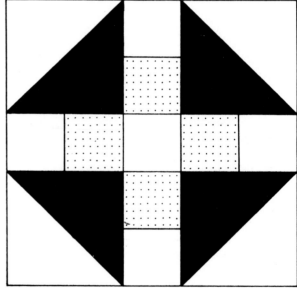

Piecing diagram c

QUILTING

1. Mark the quilting lines as shown in the quilting diagram, referring to the general quilting directions on pg. 15 if necessary.

2. Sandwich and baste the backing, batting, and patchwork top together as before.

3. Quilt along the marked lines.

FINISHING

1. Remove the basting stitches.

2. Trim the excess batting and backing evenly with the quilted top.

3. Pin and stitch the two 13½"-long binding strips to parallel edges on the Churn Dash block (see pg. 31).

4. Repeat step 3 with the two 14½"-long binding strips on the remaining edges.

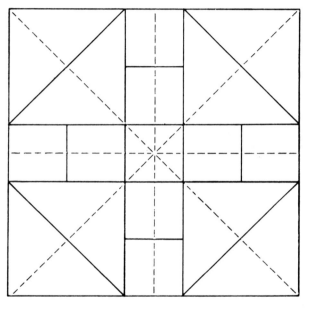

Quilting diagram

5. Maple Leaf: Piecing with a Touch of Appliqué

NATURE HAS OFTEN INSPIRED quiltmakers to translate its beauty into a patchwork pattern. Perhaps the very naturalistic Maple Leaf pattern was designed by someone who wished to capture forever the sight of the first new leaves of spring or the brilliance of autumn leaves falling to the ground. Although the design itself is very simple, the use of four different colors gives the Maple Leaf the illusion of greater complexity. Here is your first opportunity to experiment with shading as well as contrast. To help you choose your color scheme, keep in mind that leaves, as they appear in nature, are seldom one flat color. For example, a brown leaf might still have some traces of green. Don't hesitate to experiment with different colors and prints. Often, an unlikely combination has a very beautiful and dramatic effect.

The Maple Leaf pattern presents another challenge to the beginner—an introduction to appliqué. All the patterns discussed so far have been patchwork patterns. Appliqué patterns are pictorial rather than geometric. They are designed from shapes which realistically depict such things as flowers, vines, leaves, birds, and berries. These shapes are applied onto another shape or onto a large background square. Since appliqué work is quite different from patchwork, you might already have assumed that some of the preparation and construction methods will also be very different. Included below are the changes which apply to appliqué.

TOOLS

Assemble all the template and sewing supplies listed on pgs. 10-12. You needn't add anything extra for appliqué work.

FABRIC

Work with 100% cotton fabric only. Cotton is very easy to handle and will hold a crisp fold when the raw edges are turned under. Remember to prepare the fabric in the same way as before.

A 12" (completed size) Maple Leaf block requires:

1. ¼ yard each of 45"-wide pre-washed cotton fabric, colors #1, #2, and #3;

2. Enough pre-washed cotton fabric for a 4½" square, color #4;

3. ½ yard of 45"-wide pre-washed unbleached muslin or other cotton fabric for backing;

4. ¼ yard of 45"-wide pre-washed cotton fabric, any of the above colors, for binding;

5. Polyester batting.

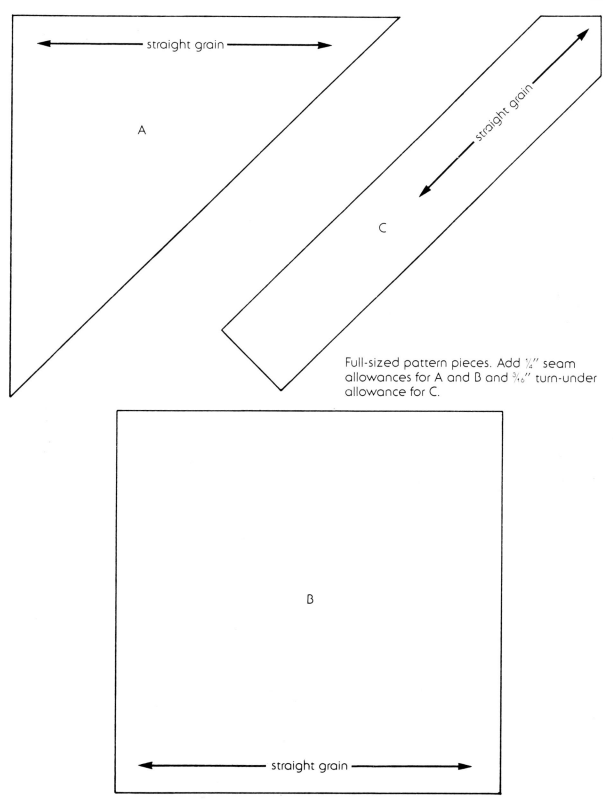

Full-sized pattern pieces. Add ¼" seam allowances for A and B and ³⁄₁₆" turn-under allowance for C.

TEMPLATES

Use the same method for drawing and cutting appliqué templates as you did for patchwork templates. Remember, each different shape requires its own template. Appliqué templates are also the exact size of the completed shape; therefore, approximately ³⁄₁₆" turn-under allowance must be added around the entire shape while marking and cutting the fabric.

For the Maple Leaf block, make one template each from the full-sized pattern pieces A, B, and C. Refer to the general instructions on pgs. 12-13 if necessary.

MARKING AND CUTTING THE FABRIC

Appliqué shapes are marked on the *right side* of the fabric. Instead of a seam line, a turn-under line is marked. If this line appears on the right side of the fabric as it should, turning under the raw edges will be easier.

A #2 lead pencil or a dressmaker's pencil is used for marking around the template. This marker should always be tested to be sure that it won't show through or bleed onto the fabric if the material gets wet.

Working on the straight grain of the fabric is not as crucial in appliqué as it is in patchwork. Actually, bias grains are easier to turn under than straight grains. Some shapes, such as leaves, will be easier to work with if the longest part is placed on the bias grain line. This, however, is not a strict rule. It is perfectly all right to place the appliqué template along the straight grain of the fabric.

The templates are marked around just as they are for patchwork. About ½" should be left between each marked piece to provide for the turn-under allowance. The shapes are then cut apart as before.

The background piece to which an appliqué is sewn must be marked to indicate its final position. The diagram of the completed pattern you are working with should be consulted and then a guideline lightly pencilled to help position the appliqué correctly. Detailed instructions for appliqué placement will be provided on an individual basis in subsequent appliqué chapters.

For the Maple Leaf block, mark and cut the patchwork pieces in the usual manner as described on pgs. 13-14. Remember, piece C is an appliqué, so it must be marked on the *right side* of the fabric. The Maple Leaf block requires:

1. 4 A pieces, color #1;
2. 4 A pieces, color #2;
3. 3 B pieces, color #3;
4. 1 B piece, color #1;
5. 1 B piece, color #4;
6. 1 C piece, color #2;
7. 2 binding strips, 13½" long by 2" wide, any color;
8. 2 binding strips, 14½" long by 2" wide, any color;
9. 13½" square for backing;
10. 13½" square of batting.

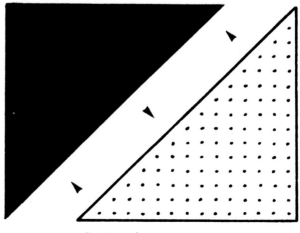

Piecing diagram a

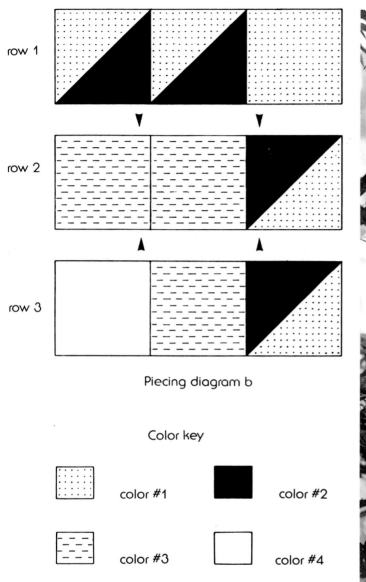

row 1

row 2

row 3

Piecing diagram b

Color key

color #1

color #2

color #3

color #4

PIECING ORDER

The Maple Leaf is constructed similarly to the Nine-Patch. Three rows of three squares each form the entire block with only four of the squares pieced from smaller units. The appliqué stem is added after the patchwork has been completed. Arrange the cut patches as shown in piecing diagrams a and b, referring to these diagrams while pinning and stitching.

PINNING AND STITCHING

There are appliqué techniques which need discussion before proceeding to pin and stitch the pieces of the Maple Leaf block.

First, any sharp curves must be clipped to make turning the raw edges easier. On any appliqué, the turn-under allowance is clipped through, just to the marked line, not through it. Then, from the *right side* of the fabric, the raw edges are turned under exactly on the marked line. The fabric is firmly pinched to crease it. As this is done, small basting stitches are taken to close the fold. Basting will keep the raw edges folded under while the shape is actually being appliquéd to the background. Any excess bulk must then be carefully trimmed away, especially at points where the turn-under allowances tend to bunch up and peek out.

The prepared appliqué is then held into place temporarily by either pinning and then basting or by lightly gluing with the glue stick. Last, a fine quilting needle (#7 or #8 Between) is threaded with a color thread that matches the appliqué, not the background. All-cotton or cotton-covered polyester thread should be used. The appliqué is stitched down using the blind-stitch, a stitch that will be explained in the following section.

With this basic knowledge of appliqué techniques, you are now ready to proceed with the construction of the Maple Leaf block.

Pin and stitch the patchwork pieces together following the same method described for the Nine-Patch and Pinwheel blocks.

1. Pin and stitch the A pieces, colors #1 and #2, into four square units (see piecing diagram a).

2. Pin and stitch the pieced squares and the B pieces into three rows (see piecing diagram b).

3. Join the rows together to form the completed block.

4. Prepare piece C for appliqué. First, fold down and baste one long edge (fig. a) to the first point. Fold, finger press, and baste this short edge to the next point (fig. b). Trim any excess bulk that tends to bunch

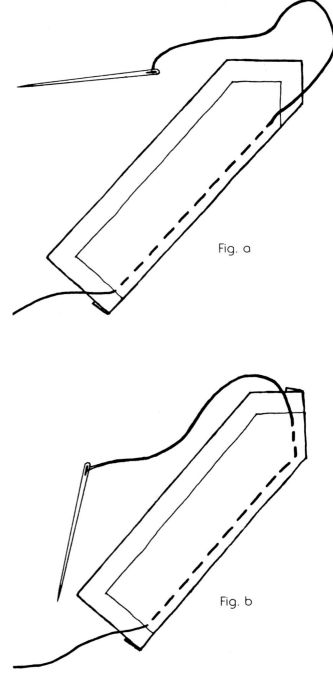

Fig. a

Fig. b

up or peek out. Fold, finger press, and baste the next point in the same manner (fig. c). Continue in this way around the entire piece C (figs. d and e).

5. Using a ruler, lightly pencil a diagonal guideline on the patch to which piece C will be appliquéd (see appliqué diagram).

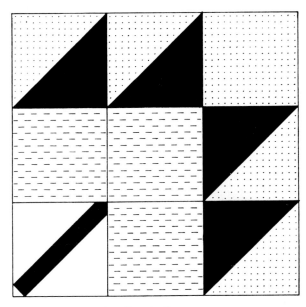

Appliqué diagram

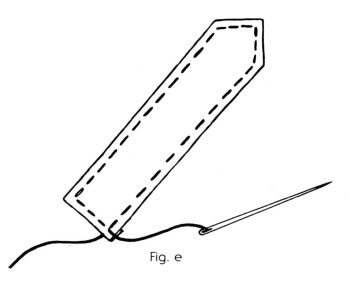

Fig. e

6. Center piece C over the guideline and either pin and baste or lightly glue into place temporarily (see fig. f).

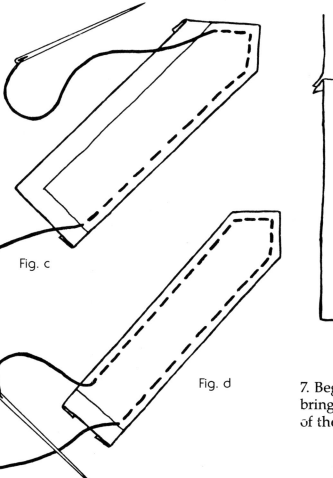

Fig. c

Fig. d

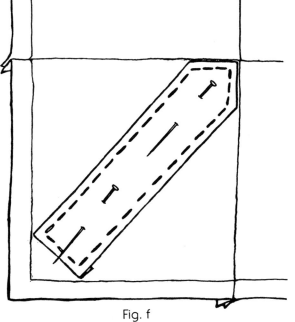

Fig. f

7. Begin stitching in the lower corner by bringing the needle up from the back side of the work, piercing the appliqué very

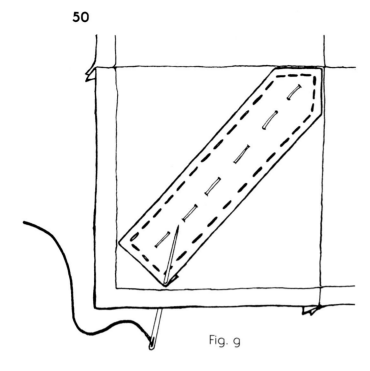

Fig. g

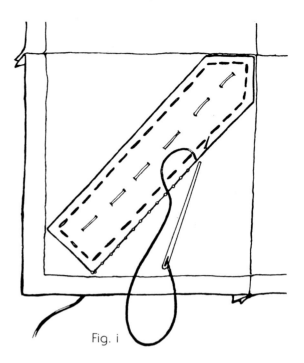

Fig. i

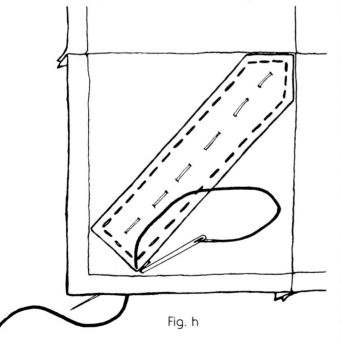

Fig. h

close to the folded edge (fig. g). Put the needle through the background fabric just above the point where the thread emerges from the appliqué (fig. h). Again, bring the needle up from the back, through the folded edge of the appliqué, but this time about ¹⁄₁₆" away from the first stitch. Continue stitching in this manner around the entire piece (see fig. i). Try to keep the stitches that appear on the top as small as possible so that they are almost invisible or "blind". Catch about ¹⁄₁₆" of background fabric in the needle so that the stitches on the back side appear longer than on the top. Place stitches closer together at the points to keep them firmly in place. End the stitching by knotting as before, but on the back side of the work.

8. Carefully remove the basting stitches.

9. Press the seam allowances and the top side of the completed Maple Leaf block.

QUILTING

1. Mark the quilting lines as shown in the quilting diagram. Refer to the instructions on pg. 15 if necessary.

2. Sandwich and baste the backing, batting, and patchwork top together.

3. Quilt along the marked lines.

FINISHNG

1. Remove the basting stitches.

2. Trim the excess backing and batting evenly with the patchwork top.

3. Pin and stitch the two 13½″-long binding strips to parallel edges on the completed block. Refer to instructions on pg. 31.

4. Repeat step 3 with the 14½″-long binding strips on the remaining edges.

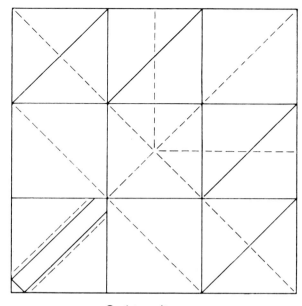

Quilting diagram

6. Basket: Piecing with Curved Appliqué

EARLY PATCHWORKERS, inspired by the simple beauty of ordinary household baskets, created an abundance of lovely basket patterns. Some are very plain, while others are very ornate, brimming with flowers, fruit, or leaves. These time-honored designs are as fresh and appealing today as they were years ago.

Simple patchwork and appliqué techniques are used to construct this Basket pattern. Choose a color scheme, either realistic or fanciful, to enhance the basket design. If you wish, experiment with a colored or a light, airy printed background instead of the usual white background. Remember, the color possibilities are limited only by your own imagination.

TOOLS

Assemble all the template and sewing supplies listed on pgs. 10-12.

FABRIC REQUIREMENTS

A 12″ (completed size) Basket block requires:

1. ¼ yard of 45″-wide pre-washed cotton fabric, color #1;

2. ½ yard of 45″-wide pre-washed cotton fabric, color #2;

3. Scrap of pre-washed cotton fabric, color #3;

4. ½ yard of 45″-wide pre-washed un-bleached muslin or other cotton fabric for backing;

5. Polyester batting.

TEMPLATES

Prepare one template each from the full-sized pattern pieces A, D, and E. Refer to the general directions on pgs. 12-13 if necessary.

Making templates for pieces B and C is optional. If you choose not to make templates for these pieces, measure and draw the dimensions provided in piecing diagram b directly onto the fabric, following the instructions on pgs. 12-13. Remember to add the usual ¼″ seam allowance on all sides of each piece just as you would when using a template.

MARKING AND CUTTING THE FABRIC

Mark and cut the fabric in the usual manner, referring if needed to the general instructions on pgs. 13-14. Remember that pieces D and E are for appliqué, so you must mark and cut on the *right side* of the fabric. The Basket block requires:

1. 1 A piece, color #1;
2. 1 A piece, color #2;
3. 2 B pieces, color #2;
4. 2 C pieces, color #2;
5. 2 D pieces, color #1;
6. 1 E piece, color #3;
7. 2 binding strips, 13½" long by 2" wide, color #2;
8. 2 binding strips, 14½" long by 2" wide, color #2;
9. 13½" square for backing;
10. 13½" square of batting.

Color key

 color #1

color #2

 color #3

PIECING ORDER

The Basket pattern is constructed in three rows. Row 2 is actually the only row requiring piecing from smaller patches into

54

Full-sized patterns pieces D and E. Add ³⁄₁₆″ turn-under allowances.

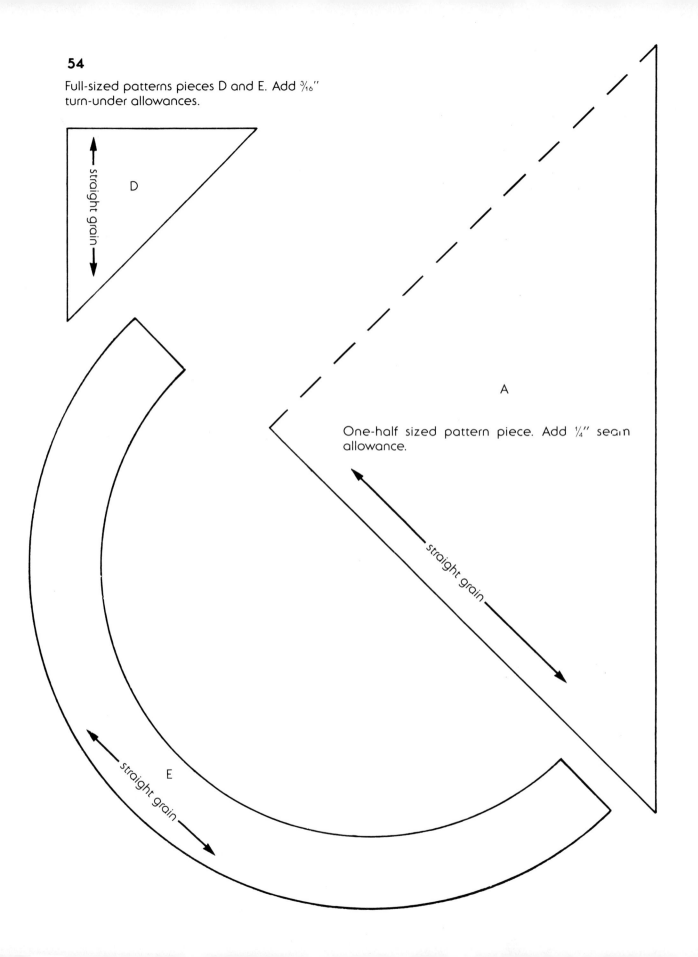

straight grain

D

A

One-half sized pattern piece. Add ¼″ seam allowance.

straight grain

straight grain

E

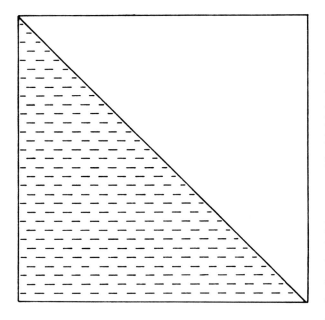

Piecing diagram a

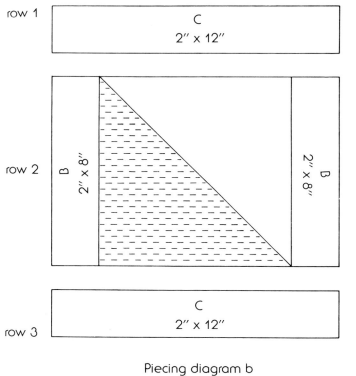

Piecing diagram b

units (see piecing diagram b). Rows 1 and 3 are simply long strips attached to either side of row 2 (see piecing diagram b). The three appliqué pieces are then added to the pieced top to complete the block (see piecing diagram c). Arrange the cut patches into their proper order, referring to the piecing diagrams as needed while pinning and stitching.

PINNING AND STITCHING

Pin and stitch the patches together using the same method as before. You may also want to refer to pgs. 47-50 for guidance on appliqué.

1. Pin and stitch the two A pieces together to form a square (see piecing diagram a).

2. Pin and stitch the two B pieces to each end of the square just made (see piecing diagram b) to form row 2.

3. Pin and stitch the two C pieces to either side of row 2 (see piecing diagram b).

4. Prepare pieces D and E for appliqué. To achieve smooth curves, clip the outer and inner curves of piece E as shown in fig. a. Sharp points on the two D pieces can be obtained using the same method described in the Maple Leaf chapter (pg. 47).

5. Position piece E on top of piece A, color

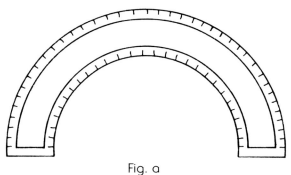

Fig. a

#2, as shown in piecing diagram c. Then pin and baste it into place. Blind stitch all around piece E.

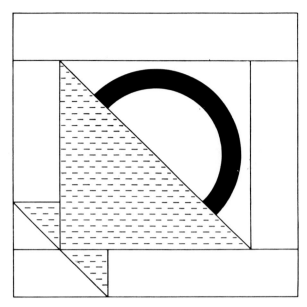

Piecing diagram c

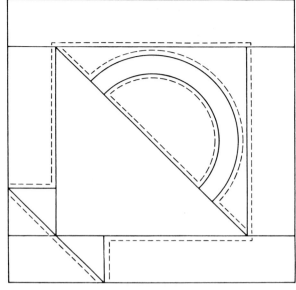

Quilting diagram

6. Repeat step 5 for the two D pieces.

7. Carefully remove all the basting stitches.

8. Press the seam allowances and the top side of the completed block.

QUILTING

1. Mark the quilting lines shown in the quilting diagram.

2. Sandwich and baste the backing, batting, and patchwork top together.

3. Quilt along the marked lines.

FINISHING

1. Remove the basting stitches.

2. Trim the excess batting and backing evenly with the patchwork top.

3. Following the method first described on pg. 31, pin and stitch the two 13½"-long binding strips to parallel edges on the completed top.

4. Repeat step 3 with the two remaining 14½"-long binding strips.

7. Schoolhouse: Building a Pictorial Block

THE SCHOOLHOUSE pattern is one of patchwork's truly pictorial designs. From this basic pattern come many variations and the many names to differentiate them. Most of these patterns are imaginary representations rather than realistic replicas of favorite schools, houses, barns, or other buildings. With this in mind, try working outside the boundaries of realism when selecting fabrics and colors—you might be happily surprised with the results. Again, you will use simple patchwork and appliqué techniques to build the Schoolhouse block.

TOOLS

Assemble the template and sewing supplies listed on pgs. 10-12.

FABRIC REQUIREMENTS

A 14" (completed size) Schoolhouse block requires:

1. Scraps or less than ¼ yard each of 45"-wide pre-washed cotton fabric, colors #1, #2, #3, and #4;

2. ½ yard of 45"-wide pre-washed unbleached muslin or other cotton fabric for background square and patchwork, color #5;

3. Additional ¼ yard of 45"-wide pre-washed cotton fabric for binding in any of the above fabrics;

4. ½ yard of 45"-wide unbleached muslin or other cotton fabric for backing;

5. Polyester batting.

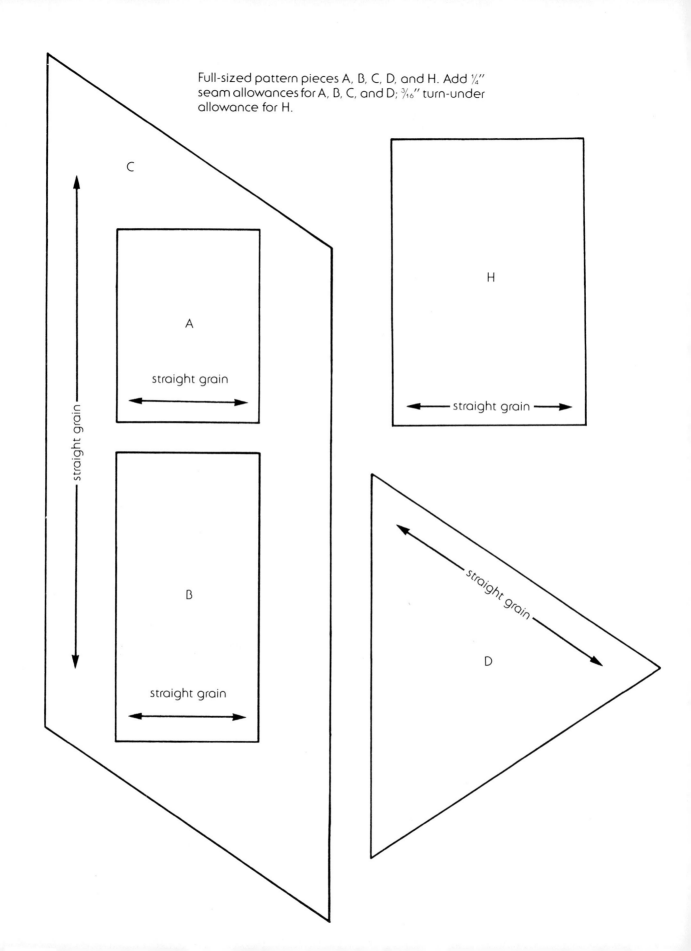

Full-sized pattern pieces A, B, C, D, and H. Add ¼"
seam allowances for A, B, C, and D; ³⁄₁₆" turn-under
allowance for H.

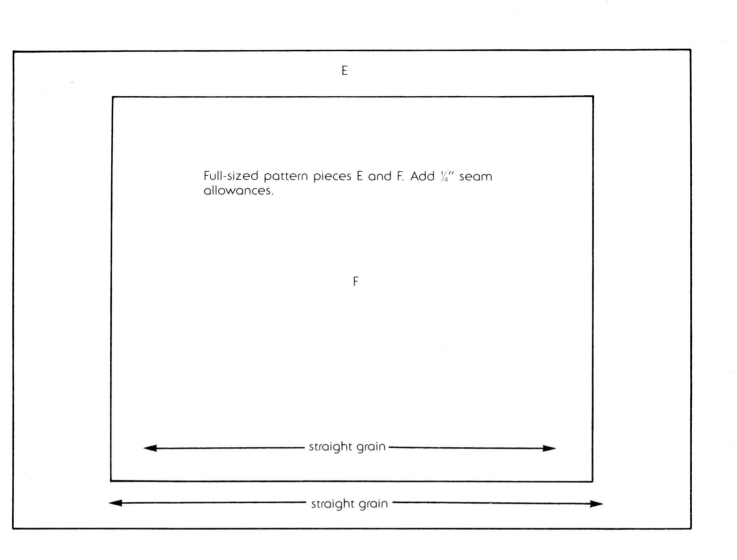

E

Full-sized pattern pieces E and F. Add ¼" seam allowances.

F

←———————— straight grain ————————→

←———————— straight grain ————————→

TEMPLATES

Make one template each from the full-sized pattern pieces A,B,C,D,E,F and H. You may either choose to make a template for G or draw this piece directly onto the fabric, using the measurements provided in the piecing diagram. Refer to the instructions for making templates on pgs. 12-13 if necessary.

MARKING AND CUTTING THE FABRIC

Mark and cut the fabric following the general instructions on pgs. 13-14 as needed. *Important:* Piece C is a non-reversible parallelogram. If you place the template for C on the wrong side of the fabric exactly as it appears in the pattern piece, you will create a mirror-image of piece C. As a result, the "roof" will face in the opposite direction it is supposed to when you piece the block together. Therefore, you must flip template C over *before* marking and cutting the fabric. It should be opposite in direction to piece C as it appears in the pattern piece. On this opposite side of template C, write *"this side up"* so you will avoid confusion and mark and cut this piece correctly. Also remember that piece H is an appliqué, so mark it on the right side of the fabric.

The Schoolhouse block requires:

1. 2 A pieces, color #1;

2. 1 B piece, color #5;

3. 1 C piece, color #1;

4. 1 D piece, color #2;

5. 1 E piece, color #3;

6. 1 F piece, color #2;

7. 1 G piece, color #4;

8. 1 H piece, color #1;

9. 2 binding strips, 15½" long by 2" wide, any color;

10. 2 binding strips, 16½" long by 2" wide, any color;

11. 14½" square for background, color #5;

12. 15½" square for backing;

13. 15½" square of batting.

Color key

 color #1

 color #2

color #3

 color #4

color #5

PIECING ORDER

The Schoolhouse block is pieced into units to form four rows (see piecing diagram), starting from the "chimneys" and working down to the "ground." Then the entire piece is appliquéd onto the 14½" back-

ground square. Refer to the piecing diagram to be certain of the correct order.

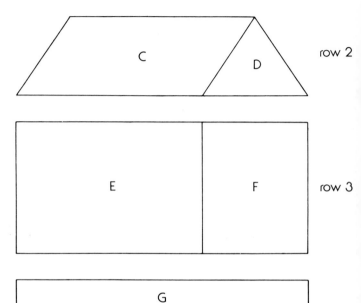

Piecing diagram

PINNING AND STITCHING

Use the familiar method for pinning and stitching the patches together first described on pgs. 22-25. You may also wish to refer to the appliqué instructions on pgs. 47-50.

1. Pin and stitch the two A pieces to each end of the B piece to form row 1.

2. Pin and stitch pieces C and D together to form row 2.

3. Pin and stitch pieces E and F together to form row 3.

4. Pin and stitch the pieced rows together,

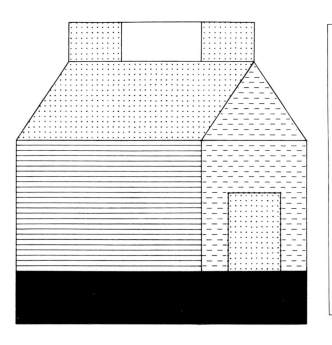

Fig. a

Fig. b

referring to the piecing diagram. Piece G forms row 4.

5. Prepare piece H for appliqué. Then pin and baste (or glue) it onto piece F (see fig. a). Appliqué H into place using the blind-stitch.

6. Press the seam allowances on the pieced section.

7. Prepare the Schoolhouse section for appliqué (see fig. b). This might be a bit more difficult than in previous projects because the turn-under line will appear on the wrong side of the fabric. As you turn under the raw edges, check from the wrong side of the fabric to see if the crease falls exactly on the marked seam lines. Baste as usual.

8. Fold the 14½″ background square in half, then in half again. Press lightly with an iron. The creases will serve as guidelines to help place the Schoolhouse squarely onto the background. Fold the Schoolhouse in half so that the chimneys meet. Finger press along the fold to mark the center. Align the center of the Schoolhouse with the vertical crease on the background square. Use a ruler to help keep all edges of the Schoolhouse equidistant from the edges of the background square.

9. Pin into position. Then baste (or use the glue stick) to hold the pieced section temporarily in place.

10. Appliqué the Schoolhouse onto the background using the blind-stitch.

11. Remove all basting stitches carefully.

12. Press the completed Schoolhouse block on the right side.

QUILTING

1. Mark the quilting lines as shown in the quilting diagram.

2. Sandwich and baste the backing, batting, and patchwork top together.

3. Quilt along the marked lines.

FINISHING

1. Remove the basting stitches.

2. Trim the excess backing and batting evenly with the patchwork top.

3. Pin and stitch the two 15½″-long binding strips to parallel edges on the completed block, referring to the general instructions on pg. 3 if necessary.

4. Repeat step 3 with the 16½″-long binding strips on the remaining edges.

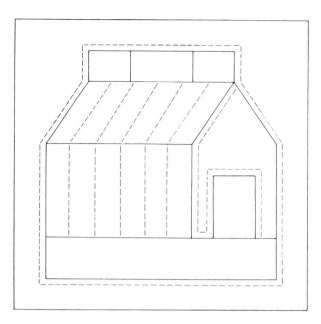

Quilting diagram

8. Amish Diamond: Diamonds in the Square

THE AMISH WOMEN of rural Pennsylvania, Ohio, and Indiana have created some of the most extraordinary quilts in America. Not only have the Amish used patchwork patterns familiar to all quiltmakers, but they have also designed patterns—such as the Amish Diamond—which are traditional only within their own communities. Expert sewing techniques and fine, intricate quilting stitches are skills for which Amish seamstresses have been admired. But it is the Amish sense of color which sets these quilts apart from all others. Solid colors are combined in bright, bold, and unusual ways. A simple quilt pattern will appear more complex because of color choice and placement.

The Amish Diamond is easily pieced, using the basic skills so far acquired. Actual color choices are provided for this pattern since an Amish sense of color is unfamiliar to many quilters.

TOOLS

Assemble the template and sewing supplies listed on pgs. 10-12.

FABRIC REQUIREMENTS

A 21″ (completed size) Amish Diamond requires:

1. less than ¼ yard each of 45″-wide pre-washed *solid* cotton fabric, medium pink, wine, and turquoise;

2. ⅜ yard of 45″-wide pre-washed solid cotton fabric, purple;

3. ½ yard of 45″-wide pre-washed solid cotton fabric, cranberry red;

4. ¾ yard of 45″-wide pre-washed solid cotton fabric for backing, medium blue;

5. Polyester batting.

TEMPLATES

Make one template each from the full-sized pattern pieces A, B, C, and D. Refer to the general instructions on pgs. 12-13 if necessary.

Pieces E, F, G, and H do not require templates. Use the measurements provided in piecing diagrams c and d to draw these pieces directly onto the fabric, following the instructions on pgs.13-14. Remember to add the usual ¼″ seam allowances just as you would if using a template.

MARKING AND CUTTING THE FABRIC

Mark and cut the fabric according to the general instructions on pgs. 13-14. The Amish Diamond requires:

1. 1 A piece, medium pink;

2. 2 B pieces, wine;

3. 2 C pieces, wine;

4. 4 D pieces, turquoise;

5. 2 E pieces, purple;

6. 2 F pieces, purple;

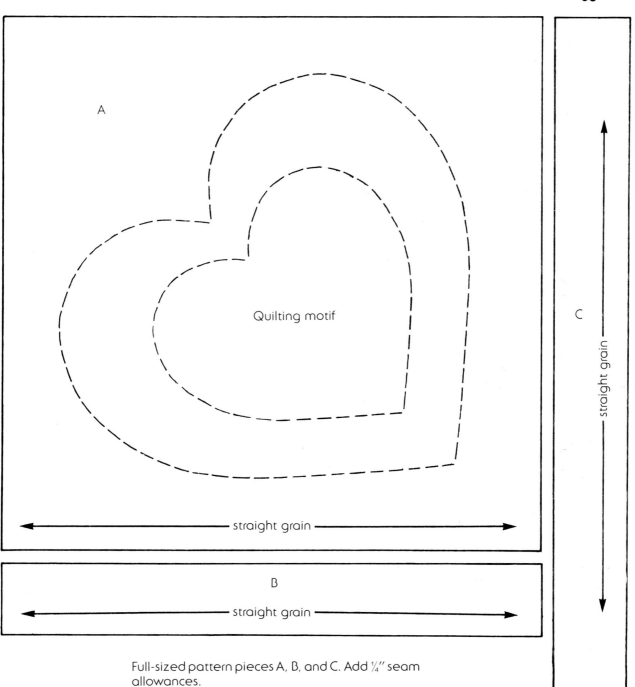

A

Quilting motif

straight grain

B

straight grain

C

straight grain

Full-sized pattern pieces A, B, and C. Add ¼" seam allowances.

7. 2 G pieces, cranberry red;

8. 2 H pieces, cranberry red;

9. 2 binding strips, 22½" long by 2" wide, purple;

10. 2 binding strips, 23½" long by 2" wide, purple;

11. 22½" square for backing;

12. 22½" square of batting.

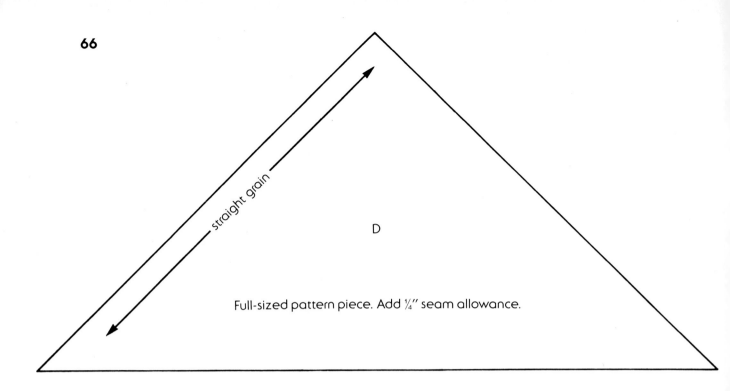

straight grain

D

Full-sized pattern piece. Add ¼″ seam allowance.

PIECING ORDER

The Amish Diamond is constructed from the center outward, rather than in rows. Arrange the cut pieces as shown in piecing diagrams a through d. Refer to these diagrams while stitching to ensure the correct piecing order.

PINNING AND STITCHING

Pin and stitch the cut pieces together, using the same method as before. Refer to the general instructions on pgs. 22-25 if necessary.

1. Pin and stitch the two B pieces to parallel edges of A (see piecing diagram a).

2. Pin and stitch the two C pieces to the remaining edges of A (see piecing diagram a again).

3. Pin and stitch one D piece to one side of the pieced A section (see piecing diagram b). Repeat with the remaining D pieces until a large square is formed.

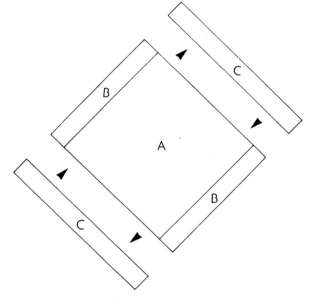

Piecing diagram a

4. Pin and stitch the two E pieces to parallel edges of the pieced square (see piecing diagram c).

5. Pin and stitch the two F pieces to the remaining edges (see piecing diagram c again).

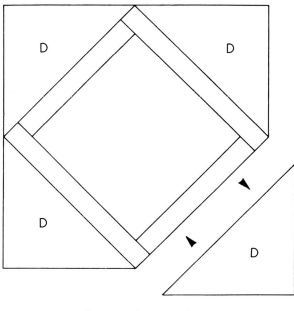

Piecing diagram b

6. Pin and stitch the two G pieces to parallel edges of the pieced square (see piecing diagram d).

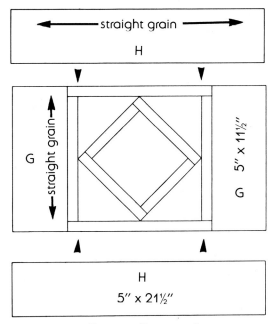

Piecing diagram d

7. Pin and stitch the two H pieces to the remaining edges (see piecing diagram d again).

8. Press the seam allowances and the top side of the completed Amish Diamond.

QUILTING

Except for the very center, all the quilting for the Amish Diamond is done "in the ditch." That is, the quilting stitches are done right in the seams of the patchwork. This eliminates the need to mark quilting lines, but it also means that the quilting stitches will be invisible from the front. However, the quilting stitches will be easily seen on the back.

The Amish Diamond is quilted with black quilting thread, a practice traditionally followed by the Amish.

1. Trace the double heart quilting motif

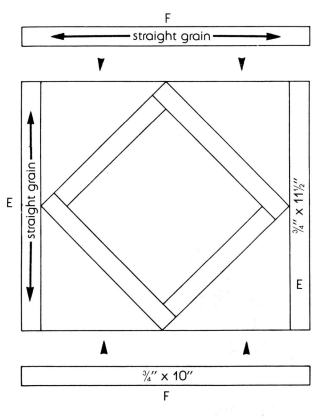

Piecing diagram c

(see pattern piece A) onto tracing paper. Place a small piece of dressmaker's carbon paper, carbon side down, on top of the center pink square. Then, place the tracing on top of the carbon paper. With a dull pencil, tracing wheel, or crochet hook, lightly re-trace the heart motif. Remove both papers to reveal the quilting lines for the double hearts. Notice that fig. b offers alternate quilting designs to choose from

Fig. a

that are equally appropriate for this area. Draw these designs directly onto the fabric using a pencil, ruler, and compass. Refer to pg. 15 for general instructions on marking quilting lines if needed.

2. Sandwich and baste the backing, batting, and patchwork top together.

3. Quilt along the marked lines and in all the seams up to and including the purple strips. Fig. a shows how the quilting stitches appear from the back.

FINISHING

1. Remove the basting stitches.

2. Trim the excess batting and backing evenly with the patchwork top.

3. Pin and stitch the two 22½"-long binding strips to parallel edges on the completed block, referring to the general instructions on pg. 31.

4. Repeat step 3 with the 23½"-long binding strips on the remaining edges.

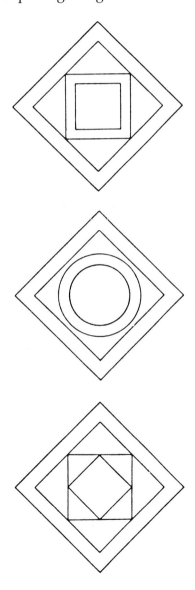

Fig. b

9. Alphabet Letters: Piecing Your Own Initials

THE PATCHWORK ALPHABET presents an opportunity for every quilter to express her individuality in a way that perhaps no other patchwork pattern does. Here the quilter has complete freedom to create a design which is hers alone. A simple initial or initials or an entire patchwork name can either stand alone or be combined with other patchwork patterns. A single pertinent word or a short message spelled out in patchwork can transform a quilted article into something unique, something which expresses the creator's own personality.

At first glance, the Alphabet Letter block might seem very complicated; but, if you analyze it carefully, you will see that it is quite simple. Each letter is constructed on a 1½" square grid system. *All* the letters are five grids (or squares) high. They differ only in width. Some letters—such as J shown here and A and B—are three grids wide. Other letters—such as G and K—are four grids wide. Finally, some letters—such as M and W—are five grids wide.

The "letter" portion of each block is formed from several individual squares in various colors and prints. The "background" portion of each block is formed from larger pieces in a light, plain fabric. The larger background pieces are formed by erasing the grid lines to create larger squares or rectangles in order to simplify piecing. Then the letter squares and the background pieces are joined into rows and/or units, according to the diagram for a particular letter.

Even if you choose to piece a letter different from the example which follows, read the directions carefully to gain a basic understanding for piecing any of the Alphabet Letter blocks.

TOOLS

Assemble all the template and sewing supplies listed on pgs. 10-12.

FABRIC REQUIREMENTS

A 13½" (completed size) Alphabet block requires:

1. Scraps of pre-washed cotton fabric, assorted prints and/or colors;

2. ¼ yard of 45"-wide pre-washed unbleached muslin or other cotton fabric, solid color for background;

3. ½ yard of 45"-wide pre-washed un-

bleached muslin or other cotton fabric for backing;

4. ¼ yard of 45″-wide pre-washed cotton fabric for binding, any color;

5. Polyester batting.

Analyze the chart for the letter J before making any templates. Keep in mind that each grid equals 1½″. First, determine how many grids (squares) wide the letter J is. Look at the chart and you will see that this letter is the standard five grids high but it is only three grids wide. Therefore, this section will measure 4½″ wide by 7½″ high when the piecing has been completed.

Next, determine how many *different* shapes are needed to construct the block for J. The chart shows that only two shapes are needed—a small square and a large rectangle. The square is equal to one grid; therefore, it will measure 1½″. The rectangle is two grids wide by three grids high; therefore, it will measure 3″ x 4½″. You will need one template for each of these shapes, using the measurements just given.

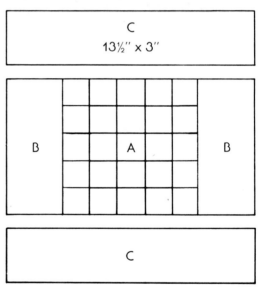

Basic piecing diagram

Now look at the basic piecing diagram for a completed Alphabet Letter block. The section labeled A represents the maximum area allowed for piecing the letters. You already know how much of this space is needed for the J (4½″ x 7½″). But, these measurements fall far short of the completed block size (13½″), so additional piecing is necessary to achieve the final dimen-

A

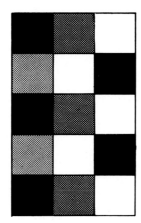

B

C

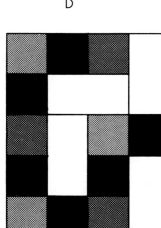

D

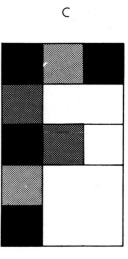

E

F

G

H

I

J

K

L

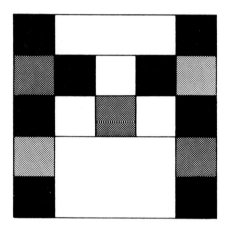

M

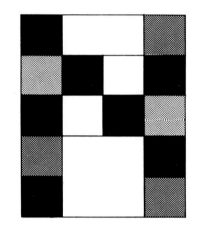

N

O

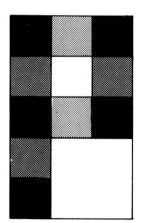

P

Q

R

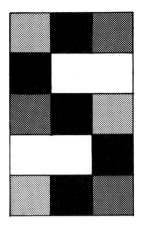

S

T

U

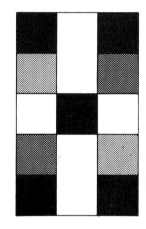

V

W

X

Y

Z

Letter Piecing Diagrams

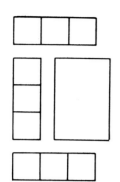

C

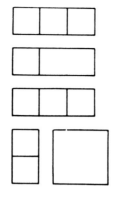

F

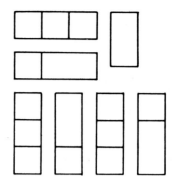

G

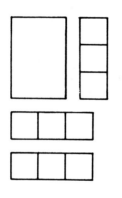

J

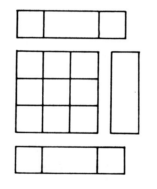

K

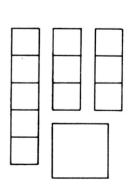

L

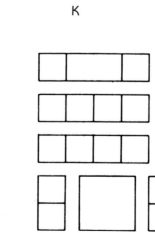

M

N

P

sions. The sections labeled B represent the pieces needed to increase the width of the A section to equal 13½". Since the J itself measures only 4½" wide (or three grids), 9" must be added to bring the total width to 13½". Therefore, two B pieces, each 4½" x 7½", must be joined to either side of the letter J to increase the width to the required 13½". One template for B, using the measurements above, will be needed.

Figuring the dimensions of the B pieces for any Alphabet Letter block is very simple. All you need to know is how many grids wide the letter you have chosen is. Then, refer to the piecing diagram. The dimensions for B vary because they are in direct proportion to the width in grids of a particular letter. Choose the correct dimensions for B according to the width of your letter and make templates as necessary. If the letter is five grids wide, the dimensions are 3" x 7½"; if four grids, 3¾" x 7½"; if three grids, 4½" x 7½".

Finally, the pieces labeled C shown in the piecing diagram are needed to increase the length of the A and B pieces to equal 13½" also. The measurements for C never vary and are provided in the basic piecing diagram.

All the Alphabet Letter blocks must be analyzed in this way before making the templates. The important factors to determine are:

1. How many grids wide a letter is;

2. How many different shapes are needed to construct the letter and what their dimensions are;

3. The measurements for the B pieces in direct proportion to the width of the letter.

TEMPLATES

After analyzing the chart for J and the basic piecing diagram, you will see that this block will require one template each for:

1. A—1½" square;

2. A1—3" by 4½" rectangle;

3. B—4½" by 7½" rectangle;

4. C—13½" by 3" rectangle (or draw directly onto the fabric).

Refer to the general instructions for making templates on pgs. 12-13 if necessary.

MARKING AND CUTTING THE FABRIC

Mark and cut the fabric in the usual manner, referring to the general instructions on pgs. 13-14 if necessary. The J block requires:

1. 8 A pieces, assorted colors and/or prints;

2. 1 A piece, solid background fabric;

3. 1 A1 piece, solid background fabric;

4. 2 B pieces, solid background fabric;

5. 2 C pieces, solid background fabric;

6. 2 strips 15" by 2" wide for binding, any color;

7. 2 strips 16" by 2" wide for binding, any color;

8. 15" square for backing;

9. 15" square of batting.

PIECING ORDER

An individual piecing diagram is provided for the letter J as well as for letters C, F, G, K, L, M, N, and P since they are also unique in composition. These special diagrams are of assistance in joining the patches together in an easy and logical way. As you will see from studying the piecing diagram for J, this block combines row piecing with unit piecing. In arranging the cut A and A1 pieces, special attention must be given to proper placement of the solid background pieces. Letters A, B, D, H, I, O, Q, R, T, U, V, W, X, Y, and Z are all simply pieced in vertical rows; letters E and S are simply pieced in horizontal rows. None of these letters require individual piecing diagrams.

PINNING AND STITCHING

Pin and stitch the patches together, using the same techniques as before. If needed, refer to the general instructions on pgs. 22-25.

1. Pin and stitch three multi-colored A pieces together to form row 1.

2. Repeat step 1 with three more multi-colored A pieces to form row 2.

3. Pin and stitch the two remaining multi-colored A pieces together with the one solid A piece in the center to form row 3.

4. Pin and stitch row 1 to piece A1 to form a large square unit.

5. Pin and stitch rows 2 and 3 together to form a rectangular unit.

6. Pin and stitch the square unit to the rectangular unit, making certain that row 3 is in the proper position (see the chart for J). The letter J itself is now complete.

7. Pin and stitch the two B pieces to either side of the completed letter (see piecing diagram).

8. Pin and stitch the two C pieces to either side of the A/B sections (see piecing diagram again).

9. Press the seam allowances and the top of the patchwork block as before.

QUILTING

1. To emphasize each letter, mark the quilting lines, in the usual manner, around the entire letter. Mark pieces B and C with a straight line about 1½″ parallel to the outside edges.

2. Sandwich and baste the backing, batting, and the patchwork top together.

3. Quilt along the marked lines.

FINISHING

1. Remove the basting stitches.

2. Trim the excess backing and batting evenly with the patchwork top.

3. Pin and stitch the two 15″-long binding strips to two parallel edges on the completed top, referring to the instructions on pg. 31.

4. Repeat step 3 with the 16″-long binding strips on the remaining edges.

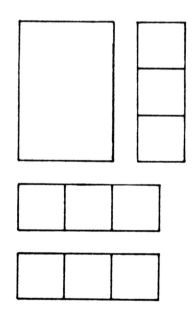

Chart for J

10. Bow-Tie: Tying An Easy Way

THE BOW-TIE is a traditional patchwork pattern which seems to capture the true spirit of patchwork. Because of its small pieces, the Bow-Tie has often been made entirely from a myriad of scraps—and in some instances, from old neckties. As a result, some very lovely and interesting examples of Bow-Tie quilts have found their place in our quilting heritage.

In its traditional form, however, the Bow-Tie can present a construction problem for the beginner. Piecing the Bow-Tie itself is simply done; but, because of the pattern's odd shapes, sewing angled seams is necessary when joining the Bow-Tie to the background pieces. This often results in unsightly puckers and much frustration for the beginner. Therefore, the Bow-Tie block presented here has been adapted for simplified piecing, but maintains the same effect as the traditional pattern.

You may choose to piece the Bow-Tie from scraps for an old-time look or from newly purchased yardage for a more refined look. Keep in mind, though, that good contrast between fabrics is needed to enhance the design.

TOOLS

Assemble the template and sewing supplies listed on pgs. 10-12.

FABRIC REQUIREMENTS

A 7½″ (completed size) Bow-Tie block requires:

1. Scraps or less than ¼ yard each of 45″-wide pre-washed cotton fabric, colors #1 and #2;
2. ⅜ yard of 45″-wide pre-washed unbleached muslin or other cotton fabric for backing;
3. ¼ yard of 45″-wide pre-washed cotton fabric for binding, color #1 or #2 or any other coordinating fabric;

4. Polyester batting.

TEMPLATES

Prepare one template each from the full-sized pattern pieces A, B, and C. Refer to the instructions on pg. 12-13 if necessary.

MARKING AND CUTTING THE FABRIC

Mark and cut the fabric in the usual manner, following the instructions on pgs. 13-14. The Bow-Tie block requires:

1. 2 A pieces, color #1;
2. 2 B pieces, color #2;
3. 2 C pieces, color #2;

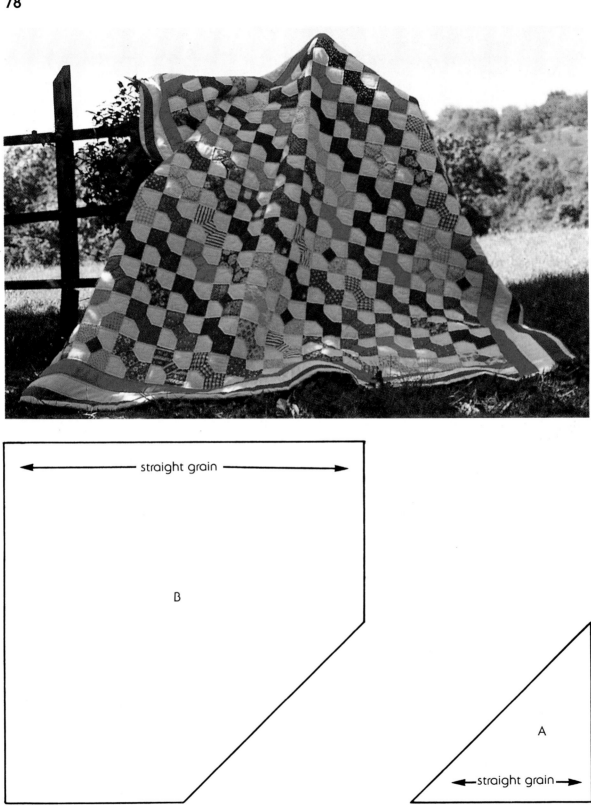

straight grain

B

A

straight grain

Full-sized pattern pieces A and B. Add ¼" seam allowances.

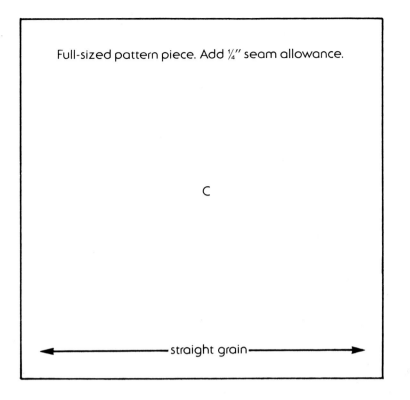

Full-sized pattern piece. Add ¼″ seam allowance.

C

←———————— straight grain ————————→

4. 2 binding strips 9″ long by 2″ wide, any color;

5. 2 binding strips 10″ long by 2″ wide, any color;

6. 9″ square for backing;

7. 9″ square of batting.

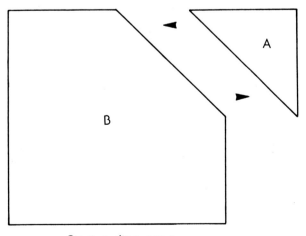

A

B

Piecing diagram a

PIECING ORDER

The Bow-Tie is constructed from simple units which are then joined into two rows. Arrange the cut patches as shown in piecing diagrams a and b, referring to these diagrams as you stitch.

PINNING AND STITCHING

Pin and stitch the patches together using the same techniques as before. Refer to pgs. 22-25 if necessary.

1. Pin and stitch one A piece to one B piece to form a square (see piecing diagram a). Repeat with the remaining A and B pieces.

2. Pin and stitch each A/B unit to one C piece to form two rows. Make certain that the A/B units are in the correct position (see piecing diagram b).

3. Join row 1 and row 2 together (see piecing diagram b again).

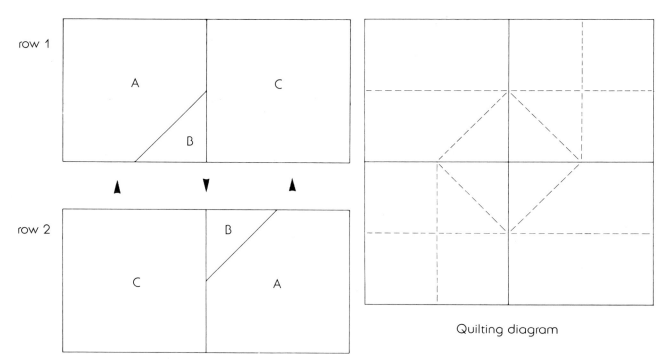

row 1

row 2

Piecing diagram b

Quilting diagram

4. Press the seam allowances and the top side of the completed Bow-Tie block.

QUILTING

1. Mark the quilting lines as shown in the quilting diagram, referring to the instructions on pg. 15.

2. Sandwich and baste the backing, batting, and patchwork top together.

3. Quilt along the marked lines.

FINISHING

1. Remove the basting stitches.

2. Trim the excess backing and batting evenly with the patchwork top.

3. Pin and stitch the two 9"-long binding strips to parallel edges on the completed block.

4. Repeat step 3 with the 10"-long binding strips on the remaining edges.

11. Sailboat: Sailing Through Simple Appliqué and Piecing

THE SAILBOAT is a non-traditional pattern whose originality demonstrates how well patchwork adapts to more contemporary themes. Its design seems to capture the excitement experienced by many sailing enthusiasts as the small, brightly colored craft skims through the water on a steady wind.

Even though the Sailboat is pictorial, prints and solids will work equally well. Solids, of course, will seem more realistic, while prints will appear more whimsical. The fabric used for the background can play an important role in suggesting certain moods or atmospheric conditions. For example: light gray might depict an overcast sky; or a light print might suggest clouds or wind. As always, use your imagination and experiment with different colors and prints. The possibilities are many.

TOOLS

Assemble the template and sewing supplies listed on pgs. 10-12.

FABRIC REQUIREMENTS

A 12″ (complete size) Sailboat block requires:

1. Scraps or less than ¼ yard each of 45″-wide pre-washed cotton fabrics, colors #1 through 5;

2. ¾ yard of 45″-wide pre-washed unbleached muslin or other cotton fabric for background, backing, and binding;

3. Polyester batting.

TEMPLATES

Following the method described on pgs. 12-13, prepare one template each from the full-sized pattern pieces A through E.

Similar to the Schoolhouse pattern in Chapter 7, the Sailboat also contains *non-reversible* shapes. The templates for pieces A through D must be turned over *before* marking the fabric to prevent making mirror-images of these shapes. The elements of the stitched sail will then appear exactly as they do in the pattern pieces. Label the reverse sides of templates A through D *this side up* to lessen confusion while marking.

MARKING AND CUTTING THE FABRIC

Mark and cut the fabric in the usual manner, referring to the instructions on pgs. 13-14. (Keep in mind that E is an appliqué and should be marked on the *right side* of the fabric.) The Sailboat requires:

1. 1 A piece, color #1;

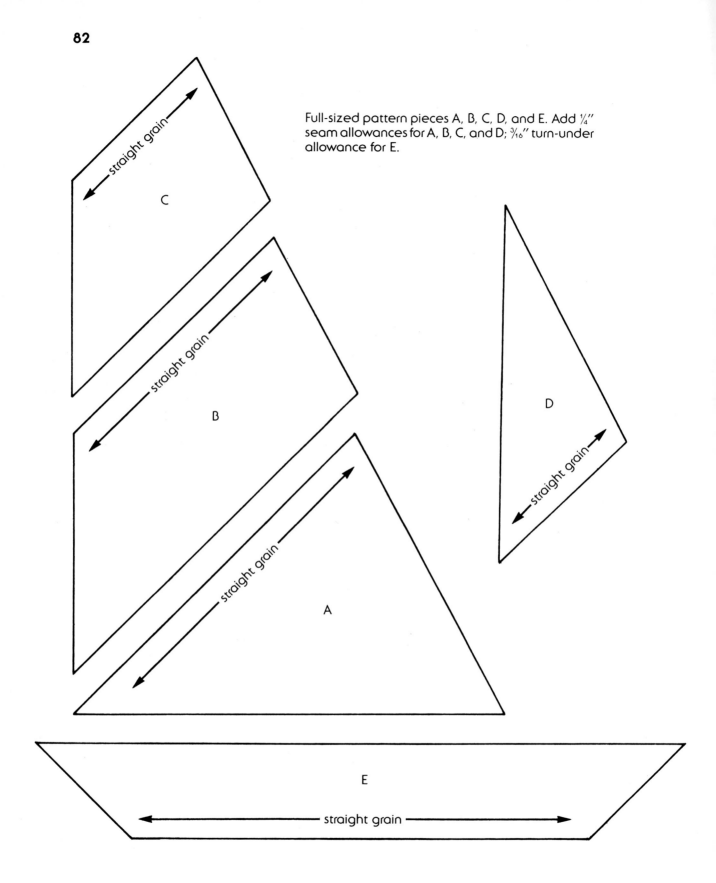

Full-sized pattern pieces A, B, C, D, and E. Add ¼"
seam allowances for A, B, C, and D; ³⁄₁₆" turn-under
allowance for E.

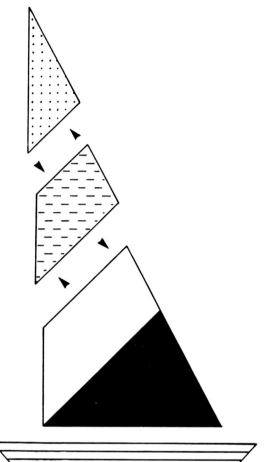

Piecing diagram a

2. 1 B piece, color #2;

3. 1 C piece, color #3;

4. 1 D piece, color #4;

5. 1 E piece, color #5;

6. 12½″ square for background, muslin or other cotton fabric;

7. 13½″ square for backing, muslin or other cotton fabric;

8. 2 binding strips 13½″ long by 2″ wide, muslin or other cotton fabric;

9. 2 binding strips 14½″ long by 2″ wide, muslin or other cotton fabric;

10. 13½″ square of batting.

Color key

■ color #1		□ color #2	

color #3

color #4

color #5

PIECING ORDER

Arrange the cut patches as shown in piecing diagram a. First the sail is pieced together. Then the sail and the hull are appliquéd onto the background square.

PINNING AND STITCHING

Pin and stitch the patches together, using

the techniques described on pgs. 22-25. You may also want to refer to the appliqué instructions on pgs. 47-50.

1. Beginning at the bottom of the sail, pin and stitch pieces A and B together; then, add C and D (see piecing diagram a). Press the seams all in one direction.

2. Prepare the sail and piece E for appliqué.

3. Fold the 12½" background block in half lengthwise, then in half again, also lengthwise. Press the folds lightly to crease. Open the fabric out flat.

4. Place the right-angle edge of the sail along the first crease on the left-hand side of the background block (see piecing diagram b). Pin and baste (or lightly glue) into place. Center piece E (the hull) underneath the sail, leaving about ¼" of the background showing between these two sections. Pin and baste (or lightly glue) into place.

5. Blind-stitch around all edges of the sail

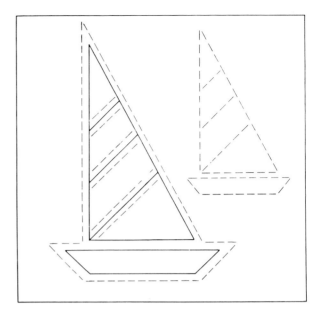

Quilting diagram a

and hull. Remember, use a separate color thread to match each different fabric.

6. Remove all basting stitches.

7. Press the completed block lightly to remove any wrinkles and creases.

QUILTING

1. Mark the quilting lines around the entire boat as shown in the quilting diagram a. Refer to the outline quilting instructions on pg. 15.

2. Trace the full-sized quilting motif provided in quilting diagram b. Put a sheet of dressmaker's carbon paper underneath the tracing and then place both (carbon side down) on the background square just to the right of the patchwork sailboat (see the quilting diagram again). With a dull pencil, tracing wheel, or crochet hook, retrace lightly over the quilting motif.

3. Sandwich and baste the backing, batting, and patchwork top together.

4. Quilt along the marked lines.

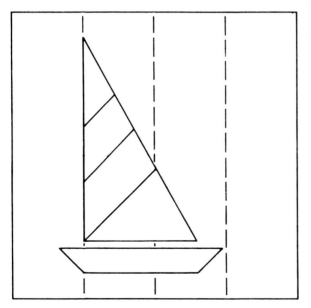

Piecing diagram b

FINISHING

1. Remove the basting stitches.

2. Trim the excess backing and batting evenly with the patchwork top.

3. Pin and stitch the two 13½"-long binding strips to parallel edges on the completed top. Refer to the instructions on pg. 31.

4. Repeat step 3 with the 14½"-long binding strips on the remaining edges.

Quilting diagram b

12. Star: Reaching for a Perfect Point

PATCHWORK STARS seem as infinite as their celestial counterparts. There are patterns which commemorate historical events, revere famous people, and honor beloved homelands. Many are elegantly simple, twinkling softly against a calm fabric sky. Others are quite complex—bursting into numerous rays of glorious color, vibrating with tremendous energy. Perhaps this diverse vocabulary of patterns reflects a special fascination quiltmakers have for this mysterious heavenly realm of which only a minute part is visible.

Even though this Star pattern uses basic construction techniques, there is one added challenge—getting the points of the twelve rays to meet properly. Because of the bulk from many seam allowances, the center is difficult to handle and the result can be a lumpy, mismatched hole instead of a fine point where all seamlines are aligned. But don't let this discourage you from trying this pattern. If you prepare the template accurately and mark the fabric with extra care, part of the challenge will be met. Exercise a little extra patience and precision while stitching. Don't hesitate to rework the center area until a satisfactory result is achieved.

The color scheme you select will have a direct influence on the overall impact of your Star quilt. For example: four shades of blue placed against a white background will produce a very soft, quiet effect. Four unrelated, but coordinating, colors placed against a tinted or printed background will create a bolder, more energetic statement. Experiment freely and creatively until the desired effect is accomplished.

TOOLS

Assemble the template and sewing supplies listed on pgs. 10-12.

FABRIC REQUIREMENTS

A completed Star quilt, measuring 43" by 47", requires:

1. ½ yard each of 45"-wide pre-washed cotton fabric, colors #1, #2, #3, and #4;

2. 1½ yards of 45"-wide pre-washed cotton fabric for background;

3. 1½ yards of 45"-wide pre-washed unbleached muslin for backing;

4. additional ½ yard of 45"-wide pre-washed cotton fabric for binding, any color #1 through #4;

5. Polyester batting.

TEMPLATES

Draw and cut one template for piece A from the full-sized pattern. Refer to the general instructions on pgs. 12-13.

MARKING AND CUTTING THE FABRIC

Mark and cut the fabric according to the methods on pgs. 13-14. For the Star quilt you will need:

Color key

color #1

color #2

color #3

color #4

1. 6 A pieces, color #1;

2. 6 A pieces, color #2;

3. 6 A pieces, color #3;

4. 6 A pieces, color #4;

5. 43½″ wide by 47½″ long rectangle, background fabric;

6. 44½″ wide by 48½″ long rectangle, backing fabric;

7. 2 binding strips, 44½″ by 2″, any color;

8. 2 binding strips, 49½″ by 2″, any color;

9. 44½″ by 48½″ rectangle of batting.

PIECING ORDER

First, the center of the Star is pieced from four pie-shaped wedges of three triangles each. Then the points are added around the outer edge of the center section. Finally, the pieced Star is appliquéd to the background.

Special care must be taken to follow the correct color sequence. Study piecing diagram a and arrange the cut patches as shown. When all the wedges have been joined together, the entire piece should follow the same order as the color key, repeating it three times.

Full-sized pattern piece. Add ¼″ seam allowance.

A

straight grain

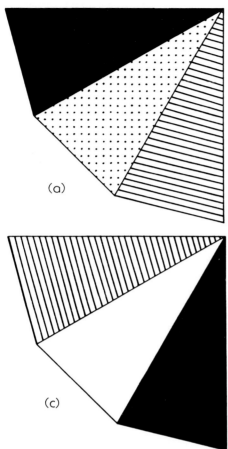

Piecing diagram a

PINNING AND STITCHING

Pin and stitch the cut patches together, using the same techniques as before. Refer to the instructions on pgs. 22-25 if necessary.

1. Pin and stitch three A pieces together to form wedge (a) as shown in piecing diagram a. Make certain that all three points meet each other precisely. Finger press the seams all in one direction, taking care not to stretch the fabric.

2. Repeat step 1 with the remaining A pieces to form wedges (b), (c), and (d).

3. Pin and stitch sections (a) and (b) together to form a half-circle (see piecing diagram b). Repeat with sections (c) and (d). Make certain to follow the proper color order.

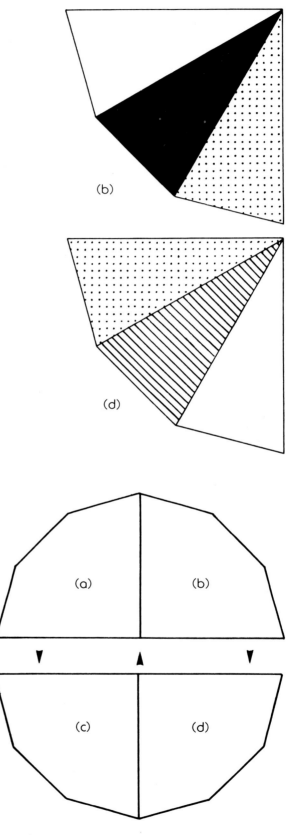

Piecing diagram b

4. Pin and stitch the a/b section to the c/d section. It may be helpful to stitch this seam in three parts. Break the stitching and begin again just before and just after the center so that this area can be easily reworked without disturbing the rest of the seam should the points not meet satisfactorily. While stitching the center section of the seam, carefully match the corresponding points on each half in the same manner used for matching corners. Keep all seam allowances free. Check the center to see how well the points meet. Rework if necessary.

5. Pin and stitch the remaining A pieces to the outer edges of the center section, matching each piece to its appropriate color mate (see piecing diagram c). Press the seam allowances toward the center section.

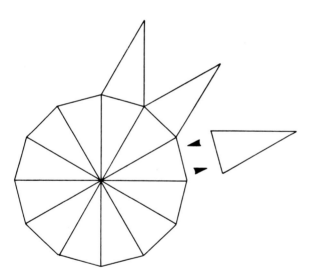

Piecing diagram c

6. Prepare the points of the Star for appliqué, referring to the instructions on pgs. 47-50 if necessary.

7. To mark the appliqué placement lines, fold the background fabric in half lengthwise then in half widthwise. Press along the fold lines. Open out the fabric.

8. Place the Star on the background and align the seam lines of each quarter section with the fold lines. The center point of each quarter section should point toward a corner of the background fabric. Measure to be certain that the Star is equidistant from the edges of the background. Pin and baste (or lightly glue) the Star into position (see fig. a).

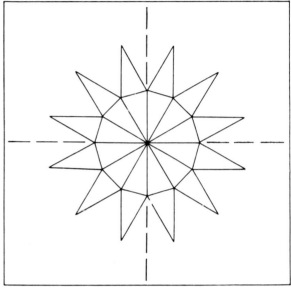

Fig. a

9. Appliqué the Star onto the background using the blind-stitch (see pg. 50). Remember, each different fabric in the Star must be sewn with a matching thread.

10. Carefully remove the basting stitches.

11. Press the completed top.

QUILTING

1. Mark the quilting lines for each quarter of the Star according to the numbered sequence shown in the quilting diagram. Refer to the instructions on pg. 15 if necessary.

2. Sandwich and baste the backing, batting, and patchwork top together.

3. Quilt along the marked lines.

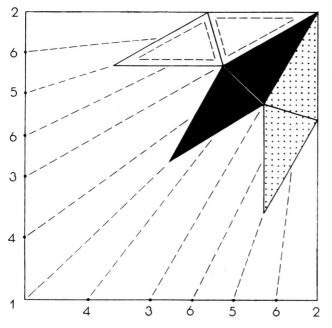

Quilting diagram (one-quarter of quilt top).

between 3 and 5 and 5 and 2 on each side toward the center;

7. Outline the inside of each pattern piece.

FINISHING

1. Remove the basting stitches.

2. Trim the excess batting and backing evenly with the completed patchwork top.

3. Pin and stitch two 44½"-long binding strips to the two shorter sides of the quilt.

4. Repeat step 3 with the two 49½"-long binding strips on the remaining edges.

The quilting lines radiate from the center of the quilt (upper right corner of the diagram).

The steps to follow for marking and quilting are:

1. Mark the first line from the lower left corner toward the center (upper right corner), to the tip of the center point;

2. Mark two lines as indicated from the upper left and lower right corners toward the center;

3. Mark two lines as indicated from the two inside seams of the three points, following a direct line from the center to the sides as marked;

4. Mark two lines as indicated equidistant between 1 and 3 on each side toward the center;

5. Mark two lines as indicated equidistant between 2 and 3 on each side toward the center to each star point;

6. Mark four lines as indicated equidistant

13. Drunkard's Path: Negotiating Curves

THE DRUNKARD'S PATH is a very old patchwork pattern with a humorous—but appropriate—name. The numerous curved seams and the almost disorderly pattern of light and dark create a confusing, dizzy effect. The patchworker seems to be following the proverbial "drunkard's path"!

Strong contrast between two colors is needed to emphasize the overall pattern of the Drunkard's Path. Many lovely antique versions were done in bright red or navy blue against a white background. With the varied palette of colors and prints available today, however, creating an equally beautiful and striking Drunkard's Path is quite easy.

TOOLS

Assemble the template and sewing supplies listed on pgs. 10-12.

FABRIC REQUIREMENTS

A 16" (completed size) Drunkard's Path block requires:

1. ¼ yard each of 45"-wide pre-washed cotton fabric, color #1 and color #2;

2. ⅝ yard of 45"-wide pre-washed unbleached muslin or other cotton fabric for backing;

3. ¼ yard of 45"-wide pre-washed cotton fabric for binding, either color #1 or #2;

4. Polyester batting.

TEMPLATES

Referring to the instructions on pgs. 12-13, prepare one template each from the full-sized pattern pieces A and B. Make certain to draw the center marks on each template.

MARKING AND CUTTING THE FABRIC

As you draw around the templates, you must also reproduce the center marks on the fabric in the designated spot. These marks are vital for the proper alignment of the two pattern pieces along the curved seam line. Otherwise, mark and cut the fabric as usual, referring to the instructions on pgs. 13-14. The Drunkard's Path block requires:

1. 12 A pieces, color #1;

2. 4 A pieces, color #2;

3. 12 B pieces, colors #2;

4. 4 B pieces, color #1;

5. 2 binding strips 17½" long by 2" wide, either color #1 or #2;

6. 2 binding strips 18½" long by 2" wide, either color #1 or #2;

7. 17½" square for backing;

8. 17½" square of batting.

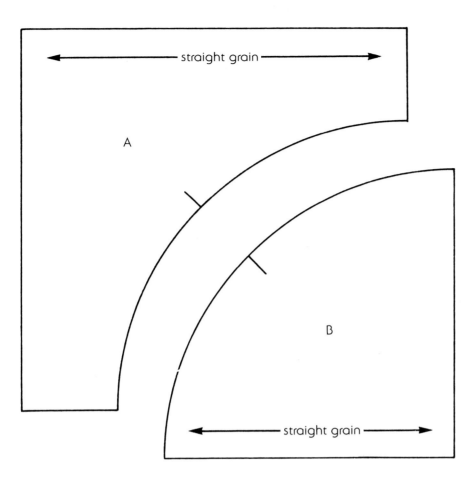

Full-sized pattern pieces A and B. Add ¼" seam allowances.

PIECING ORDER

The basic unit of the Drunkard's Path is a square consisting of one A and one B piece sewn together along the curved seam line. The squares are joined into four rows of four squares each to form the completed block. Arrange the cut A and B patches as shown in piecing diagram a, noticing that there are two different color combinations.

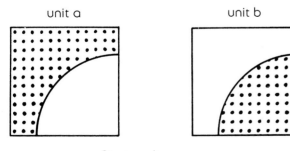

Piecing diagram a

PINNING AND STITCHING

Pin and stitch the cut patches in the following manner:

1. With the right sides facing each other, place one A piece, color #1, and one B piece, color #2, together along the curved edges (see piecing diagram a). Place a pin in the right-hand corners of both pieces,

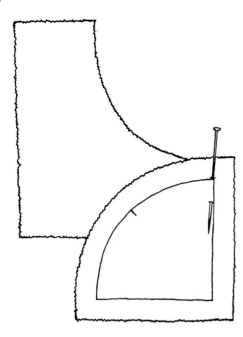

Fig. a

Fig. b

making certain to match the corners exactly. Bring the pin forward, matching the *straight* seam lines of both patches (see fig. a).

2. Repeat step 1 with the left-hand corners.

3. Place a third pin through the center marks on both pieces, matching the curved seam lines exactly (see fig. b).

4. Place two additional pins along the curved seam line, one on either side of the

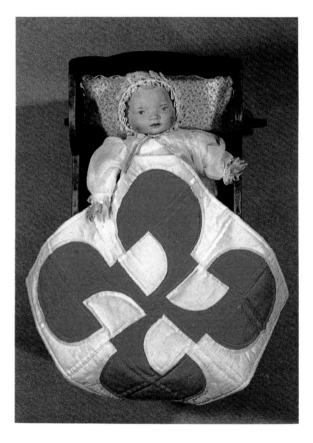

center pin. The fabric will curl up between the pins, making it seem as though the fabric will never lie flat enough to stitch. Don't become alarmed. Add more pins in these spots to help the fabric lie flatter, making certain to always match both sets of seam lines.

5. Stitch along the curved seam lines (see

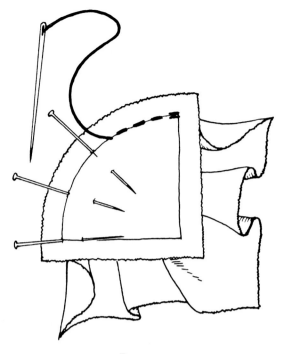

Fig. c

fig. c). Ease in any extra fullness by *gently* and *carefully* pressing the fabric between your fingers as you go or by adding more pins to help flatten the fabric. Take care not to sew in any puckers. Turn the work over occasionally to check that the stitching goes through the seam line on the bottom piece also.

6. Clip the curved seam allowances in several spots to help the pieced unit lie flat. Press the seam allowances toward piece A, being careful not to stretch the curved seam line.

7. Repeating steps 1-6, piece eleven more (a) units and four (b) units as shown in piecing diagram a.

8. Using the same method as in previous chapters, pin and stitch four (a) units together to form row 1 (see piecing diagram b). Repeat to form row 4.

9. Again following the sequences shown in piecing diagram b, pin and stitch two (a) units and two (b) units together to form row 2 and then row 3.

10. Pin and stitch the four rows together to form the completed block.

11. Press the seam allowances and the top side of the patchwork.

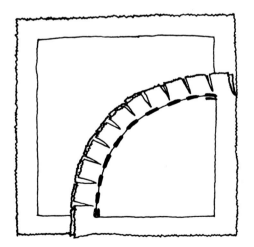

Fig. d

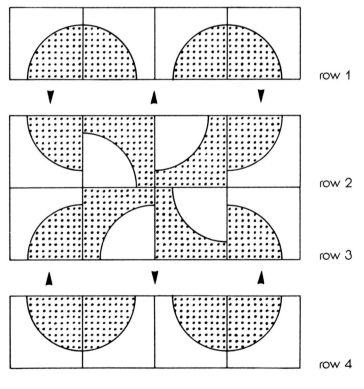

Piecing diagram b

QUILTING

1. Mark the quilting lines as shown in the quilting diagram. Refer to the instructions on pg. 15 if necessary.

2. Sandwich and baste the backing, batting, and patchwork top together.

3. Quilt along the marked lines.

FINISHING

1. Remove the basting stitches.

2. Trim the excess batting and backing evenly with the patchwork top.

3. Pin and stitch the two 17½″-long binding strips to parallel edges on the completed top.

4. Repeat step 3 with the 18½″-long binding strips on the remaining edges.

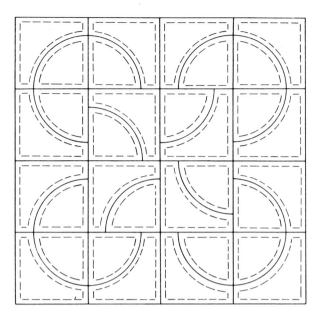

Quilting diagram

14. Fan: Piecing a Curved Line

TODAY, FANS may seem to be a quaint curiosity, but in Victorian times they were an essential part of every well-mannered, well-dressed lady's wardrobe. They provided an acceptable way to cool a properly attired—but by our standards, over-dressed—lady. Fans played an important role in the fashionable arts of flirtation and fainting, and were often used to communicate thoughts and feelings considered improper to express verbally. It is little wonder then that this once common fashion accessory served as the source of inspiration for many lovely patchwork Fan patterns.

The Fan adapts well to many color and fabric choices. A mix and match arrangement of printed scraps is just as suitable as a more planned, repetitive combination. Simply remember to select fabrics that will allow the fan to stand out against the background.

TOOLS

Assemble the template and sewing supplies listed on pgs. 10-12.

FABRIC REQUIREMENTS

A 12″ (completed size) Fan block requires:

1. Scraps or less than ¼ yard each of pre-washed cotton fabrics, colors #1, #2, #3, #4, #5;

2. ½ yard of 45″-wide pre-washed cotton fabric for background, color #6;

3. ½ yard of 45″-wide pre-washed un-bleached muslin or other cotton fabric for backing;

4. ¼ yard of 45″-wide pre-washed cotton fabric for binding, any of the above colors;

5. Polyester batting.

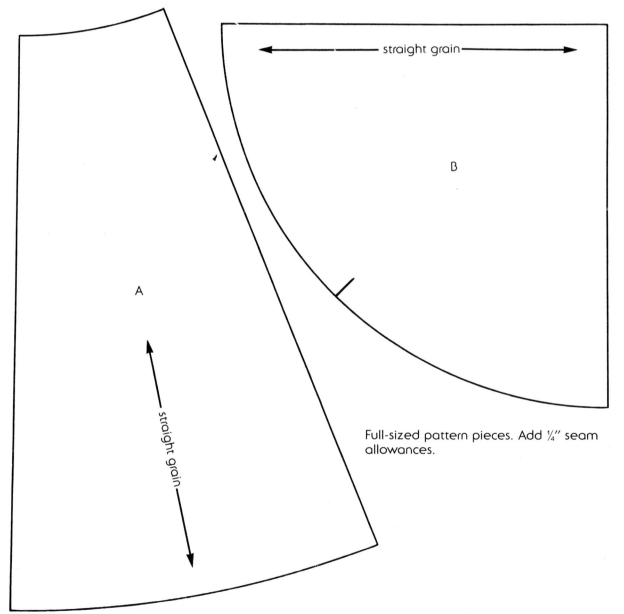

Full-sized pattern pieces. Add ¼″ seam allowances.

TEMPLATES

Prepare one template for pieces A and B from the full-sized patterns. Refer to the instructions on pgs. 10-12. Include the center mark on template B.

MARKING AND CUTTING THE FABRIC

Mark and cut the fabric according to the instructions on pgs. 13-14. The Fan block requires:

1. 1 A piece of each color #1 through #4;
2. 1 B piece, color #5;
3. 12½" square for background, color #6;
4. 2 binding strips, 13½" by 2", any color;
5. 2 binding strips, 14½" by 2", any color;
6. 13½" square for backing;
7. 13½" square of batting.

PIECING ORDER

Four A pieces are joined together to form a semicircular fan. Then, B is joined to the fan along the small curved edge. Finally, the pieced fan is appliquéd onto the background. Arrange the cut patches as shown in the piecing diagram. Refer to this diagram as you stitch.

PINNING AND STITCHING

Pin and stitch the cut patches together using the same methods as before (see pgs. 22-25).

1. Join two A pieces together along one long edge. Repeat with the remaining A pieces (see piecing diagram a). You may use any color sequence suitable to your choice of fabrics.
2. Pin and stitch piece B to the A sections, using the same techniques learned in the Drunkard's Path (see pgs. 93-95). Match the center mark on piece B to the fan's center seam line (see piecing diagram b).

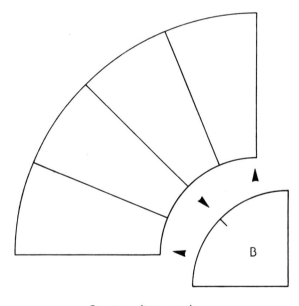

Piecing diagram b

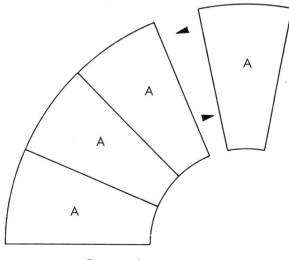

Piecing diagram a

3. Press the fan's seam allowances all in one direction. Then press the curved seam allowances toward the fan.

4. Prepare the pieced fan for appliqué only along the large curved edge. Refer to the appliqué instructions on pgs. 47-50 if needed.

5. Place the fan on the 12½" background square, keeping the straight edges of both

pieces even (see appliqué diagram). Pin and baste (or lightly glue) into place.

6. Appliqué the fan into place along the prepared edge. Remove all basting stitches. From the wrong side of the block, carefully trim away the background fabric about ¼" away from the curved appliqué stitching line. This will eliminate the extra layer of fabric underneath the fan and will allow for easier quilting. The leftover fabric can be saved for the scrap-bag.

7. Press the top side of the completed Fan block.

QUILTING

1. Mark the quilting lines as shown in the quilting diagram. Refer to the instructions on pg. 15.

2. Sandwich and baste the backing, batting, and patchwork top together.

3. Quilt along the marked lines.

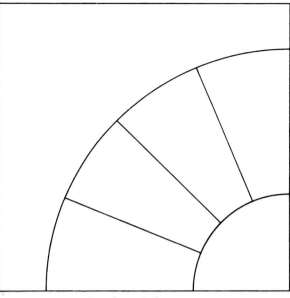

Appliqué diagram

FINISHING

1. Remove the basting stitches.

2. Trim the excess batting and backing evenly with the patchwork top.

3. Pin and stitch the two 13½"-long binding strips to two parallel edges.

4. Repeat step 3 with the 14½"-long binding strips on the remaining edges.

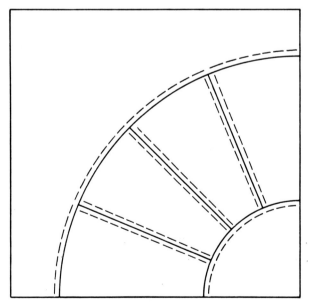

Quilting diagram

15. Dresden Plate:
A Testimony of Friendship

FRIENDSHIP QUILTS were often presented to a woman on the eve of her marriage or before setting out for unknown regions in search of a new home and better land. The Dresden Plate—with its many variations—was a popular choice for such a quilt. The scalloped

wedges were made from different scraps donated by each quilter as a special re-membrance of love and friendship.

In the spirit of this tradition, it might be very rewarding to stitch the Dresden Plate with scraps gathered from your special friends and relatives. Or, for a more refined look, the versatile Dresden Plate can be stitched from two contrasting, but coordinating, fabrics. Either choice will create a very attractive color scheme.

TOOLS

Assemble the template and sewing sup-plies listed on pgs. 10-12.

FABRIC REQUIREMENTS

A 16″ (completed size) Dresden Plate block requires:

1. Scraps of eight different prints or ¼ yard each of 45″-wide pre-washed cotton fabric, colors #1 and #2;

2. ¾ yard of 45″-wide pre-washed un-bleached muslin or other cotton fabric for background, backing, and binding;

3. Polyester batting.

TEMPLATES

Prepare one template from the full-sized pattern piece A. Refer to the instructions on pgs. 12-13.

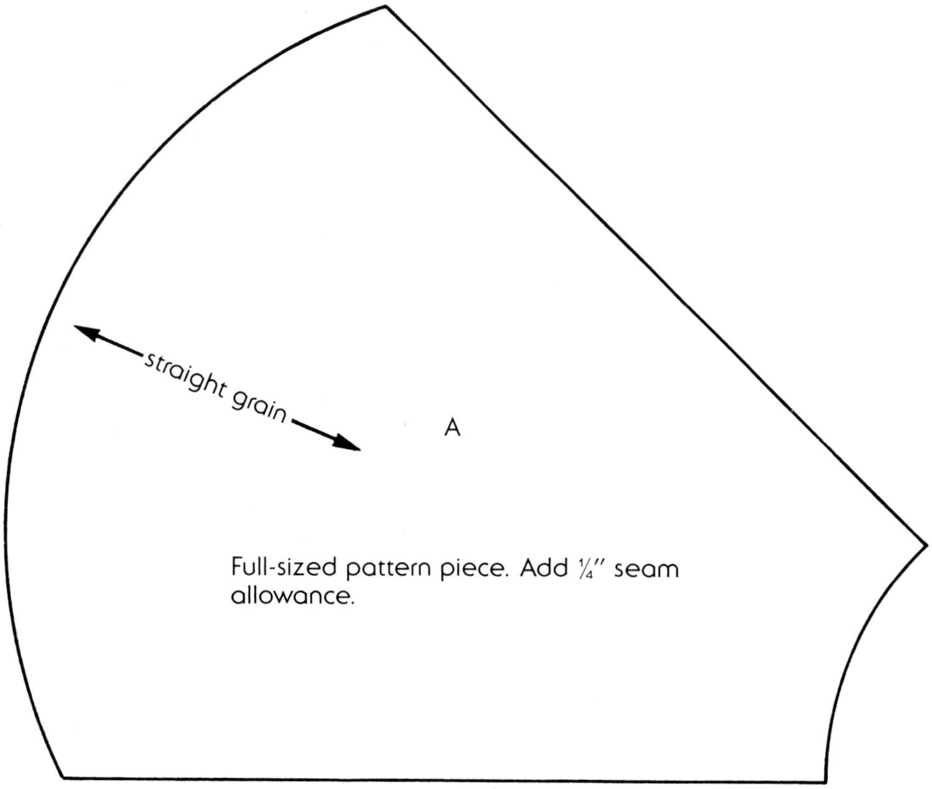

straight grain

A

Full-sized pattern piece. Add ¼″ seam allowance.

MARKING AND CUTTING THE FABRIC

Mark and cut the fabric as before. Refer to the instructions on pgs. 13-14 if necessary. The Dresden Plate block requires:

1. 8 A pieces from assorted scraps or 4 A pieces, color #1, and 4 A pieces, color #2;

2. 16½" square for background, unbleached muslin or other cotton fabric;

3. 17½" square for backing, unbleached muslin or other cotton fabric;

4. 2 binding strips 17½" long by 2" wide, muslin or other cotton fabric;

5. 2 binding strips 18½" long by 2" wide, muslin or other cotton fabric;

6. 17½" square of batting.

PIECING ORDER

Eight pie-shaped wedges are joined together to form a plate. Then the plate is appliquéd onto a large background square. If you have chosen to use all scraps, arrange them in any pleasing color sequence. When using only two coordinated fabrics, arrange them in an alternating color sequence.

PINNING AND STITCHING

Pin and stitch the cut patches together using the methods described on pgs. 22-25. You may also want to refer to the appliqué instructions on pgs. 47-50.

1. Pin and stitch two A pieces together along one common straight edge. Join the remaining A pieces one at a time to this section until a full circle has been completed (see piecing diagram).

2. Carefully press the seams all in one direction, taking care not to stretch the fabric.

3. Prepare the inner and outer curved edges for appliqué. *Helpful hint:* Place the

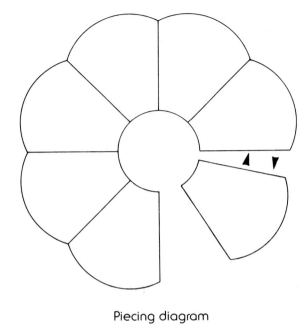

Piecing diagram

template for A on the *wrong* side of each wedge in the circle, matching the marked seam lines to the template's edge. Hold firmly in place. Then, from the *right* side, fold the turn-under allowances over the edge of the template; pinch slightly to

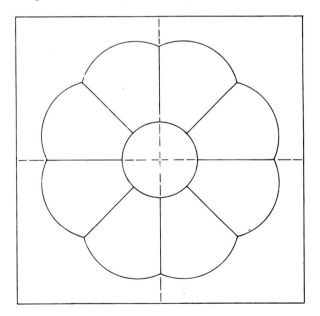

Appliqué diagram

crease. Doing this, along with careful and frequent clipping, will help you achieve smooth, uniform curves.

4. Fold the 16½" background square into four square sections. Press the folds lightly to crease. Open the fabric out flat.

5. Position the prepared plate onto the background, matching four straight seam lines to the four creases (see appliqué diagram). Pin and baste (or lightly glue) into place.

6. Blind stitch the plate into position, starting with the small inner curve, working the outer curve last. Change the thread as needed to match the individual fabrics.

7. Carefully remove all basting stitches.

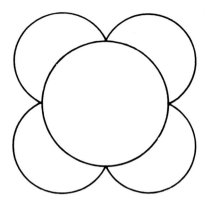

Quilting diagram b

carbon paper, transfer this motif to the center of the plate, following the same method as for the Amish Diamond (pg. 68).

3. Sandwich and baste the backing, batting, and patchwork top together.

4. Quilt along the marked lines.

FINISHING

1. Remove the basting stitches.

2. Trim the excess batting and backing evenly with the patchwork top.

3. Pin and stitch the two 17½"-long binding strips to parallel edges on the completed block.

4. Repeat step 3 with the two 18½"-long binding strips on the remaining edges.

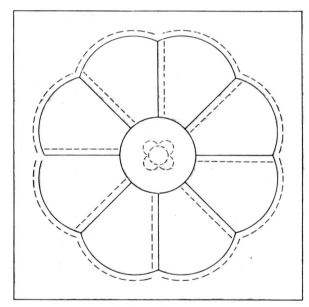

Quilting diagram a

QUILTING

1. Mark the quilting lines as shown in the quilting diagram a, following the outline quilting instructions on pg. 15.

2. Trace the full-sized quilting motif shown in quilting diagram b. Using dressmaker's

16. Wheel of Fortune: Taking a Chance on Curved Appliqué

THE WHEEL OF FORTUNE—known also as Hearts and Gizzards and Springtime Blossoms—is a very old pattern with a surprisingly modern appearance. Its petal-like wheels whirl with perpetual motion and energy, never allowing the eye to rest comfortably in one spot for very long. Perhaps it is this mesmerizing illusion which first suggested the name Wheel of Fortune. Like the carnival game—or even the game of Life—the wheel goes round and round and where it stops, only Fortune knows.

To create a strong visual impact, select two boldly contrasting fabrics. For example: any deep, rich color—such as red—when combined with white, will achieve the desired effect. Of course, any other two color combinations will work just as well. Remember though, look at your selection from a distance to check for the proper amount of contrast.

TOOLS

Assemble the template and sewing supplies listed on pgs. 10-12.

FABRIC REQUIREMENTS

A 14″ (completed size) Wheel of Fortune block requires:

1. ¼ yard 45″-wide pre-washed cotton fabric, color #1;

2. ¼ yard 45″-wide pre-washed cotton fabric, color #2;

3. ½ yard 45″-wide pre-washed unbleached muslin or other cotton fabric for backing;

4. additional ¼ yard 45″-wide pre-washed cotton fabric for binding, either color #1 or #2;

5. Polyester batting.

TEMPLATES

Prepare one template each for pieces A and B from the full-sized patterns. Refer to the template-making instructions on pgs. 12-13 if necessary.

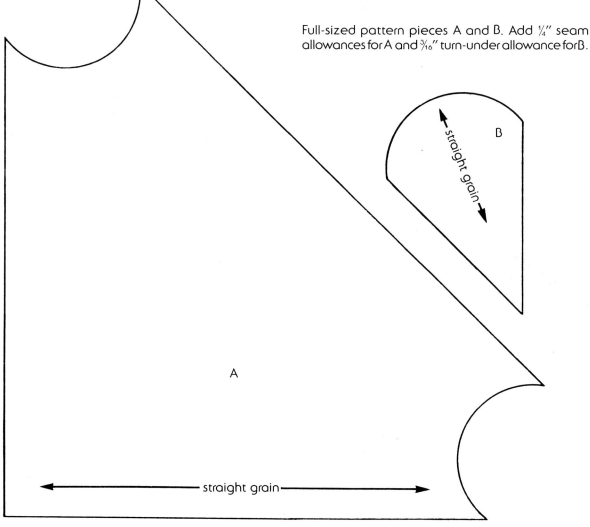

Full-sized pattern pieces A and B. Add ¼″ seam allowances for A and ³⁄₁₆″ turn-under allowance for B.

A

B

straight grain

straight grain

MARKING AND CUTTING THE FABRIC

Even though all the B pieces are appliqués, mark them on the *wrong side* of the fabric instead of the right side as you normally would for appliqué. This will allow for easier piecing in the long run. Mark and cut the fabric as usual, referring to the instructions on pgs. 13-14 if necessary. The Wheel of Fortune block requires:

1. 4 A pieces, color #1;

2. 4 A pieces, color #2;

3. 8 B pieces, color #1;

4. 8 B pieces, color #2;

5. 15½" square for backing, unbleached muslin or other cotton fabric;

6. 2 binding strips 15½" long by 2" wide, either color #1 or #2;

7. 2 binding strips 16½" long by 2" wide, either color #1 or #2;

8. 15½" square of batting.

PIECING ORDER

The Wheel of Fortune is comprised of one basic unit, but with two different color arrangements. Two of the basic units form a large square unit which, when joined into two rows of two squares each, completes the pattern.

Arrange the cut patches as shown in piecing diagram a, always referring to this diagram as you pin and stitch to ensure the correct color order.

PINNING AND STITCHING

The Wheel of Fortune combines patchwork and appliqué techniques. Refer to the patchwork instructions on pgs. 22-25 and the appliqué instructions on pgs. 47-50 if necessary.

1. Prepare only the *curved* edges of all the B patches for appliqué. To help you achieve smooth curves without points, first sew a row of basting stitches in the seam allowance close to the curve (see fig. a). Place the template for piece B on the *wrong side* of the patch, matching the marked seam lines to the template's edge. Gently

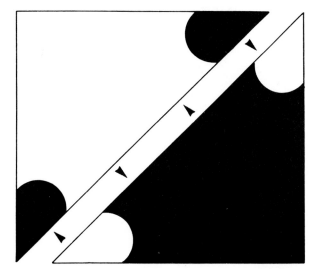

Piecing diagram a

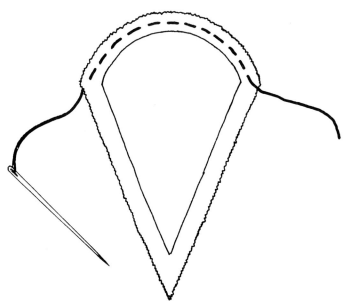

Fig. a

pull one end of the basting thread to gather the seam allowance over the edge of the template (see fig. b). Press lightly. Remove the template. Baste the folded edge as usual. Clip the seam allowances only if absolutely necessary to smooth out any points that might appear. Remove the first set of basting stitches.

2. Working on the *right side*, place the curved edge of one B piece, color #2, over one concave curve of piece A, color #1 (see fig. c). Pin the pieces together, matching the very edge of B precisely to the marked seam line which appears on the *wrong* side of piece A. It will require a little extra manipulation and patience to match these two pieces exactly. Blind-stitch piece B to piece A, matching the thread to B. Remove the basting stitches. Repeat this process with the remaining concave curve on A to complete one triangle (see piecing diagram a). Pin and stitch three more triangles in this way.

3. Pin and stitch four triangular units together in the opposite colors, following the same method described in step 2.

4. Pin and stitch two triangular units of different colors together. Repeat until you have four squares (see piecing diagram a).

5. Following the color sequence shown in piecing diagram b, pin and stitch the

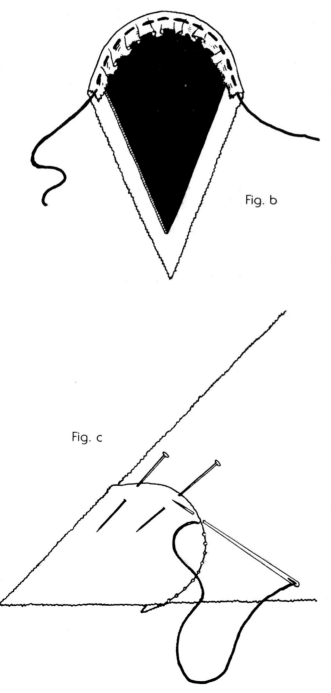

Fig. b

Fig. c

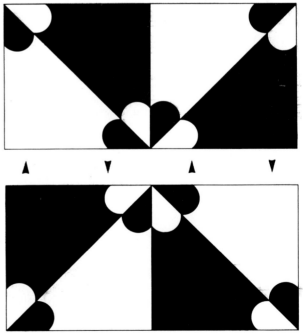

Piecing diagram b

squares into two rows of two squares each. Then join the rows together.

6. Press the seam allowances and the top side of the completed block.

QUILTING

1. Mark the quilting lines as shown in the quilting diagram, referring to the outline quilting instructions on pg. 15.

2. Sandwich and baste the backing, batting, and patchwork top together (see pgs. 14-15).

3. Quilt along the marked lines.

FINISHING

1. Remove the basting stitches.

2. Trim the excess batting evenly with the patchwork top.

3. Pin and stitch the two 15½"-long binding strips to parallel edges on the quilted block (see pg. 31).

4. Repeat step 3 with the two 16½"-long binding strips on the remaining edges.

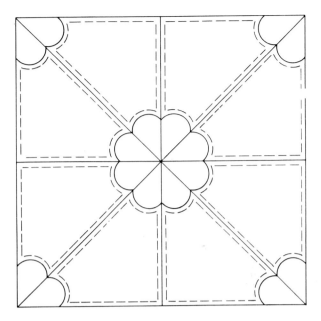

Quilting diagram

17. Wreath: Appliqué for All Seasons

LEAVES AND FLOWERS, gracefully entwined with each other, have inspired a garden full of lovely Wreath patterns. Elegant or simple, each blossoms in full glory, preserving Nature's beauty a while longer in a treasured quilt.

The all-appliqué Wreath presented here is quite simple. Its use of assorted scrap fabrics for the leaves creates a carefree, fanciful atmosphere. And it is because of its simplicity that many other color and fabric choices can be just as effective. For example: several different earth-tone fabrics might give the impression of autumn leaves. Have fun experimenting and creating different effects with this very flexible pattern.

TOOLS

Assemble the template and sewing supplies listed on pgs. 10-12.

FABRIC REQUIREMENTS

A 16" (completed size) Wreath block requires:

1. Assorted scraps of pre-washed cotton fabrics;

2. ¼ yard of 45"-wide pre-washed cotton fabric, solid green;

3. ¾ yard of 45"-wide pre-washed unbleached muslin or other cotton fabric for background, backing, and binding;

4. Polyester batting.

TEMPLATES

Prepare one template for piece A from the full-sized pattern. Refer to the instructions on pgs. 12-13. Piece B is a guide, rather than a complete pattern piece, to assist you in marking and cutting several bias strips. Prepare a guide for piece B just as you would a template, using the measurements provided.

MARKING AND CUTTING THE FABRIC

For piece A, mark and cut the fabric according to the instructions for appliqué (see pg. 46). The background and backing squares and the binding strips are marked and cut in the usual manner. Special instructions for marking and cutting piece B on the bias will follow. The Wreath will require:

1. 24 A pieces from assorted fabrics;

2. 16½" square for the background, unbleached muslin;

3. 17½" square for the backing, unbleached muslin;

4. 2 binding strips 17½" long by 2" wide, unbleached muslin;

One-half sized guide for bias strip. Do not add turn-under allowance.

| B | ¾" x 12" |

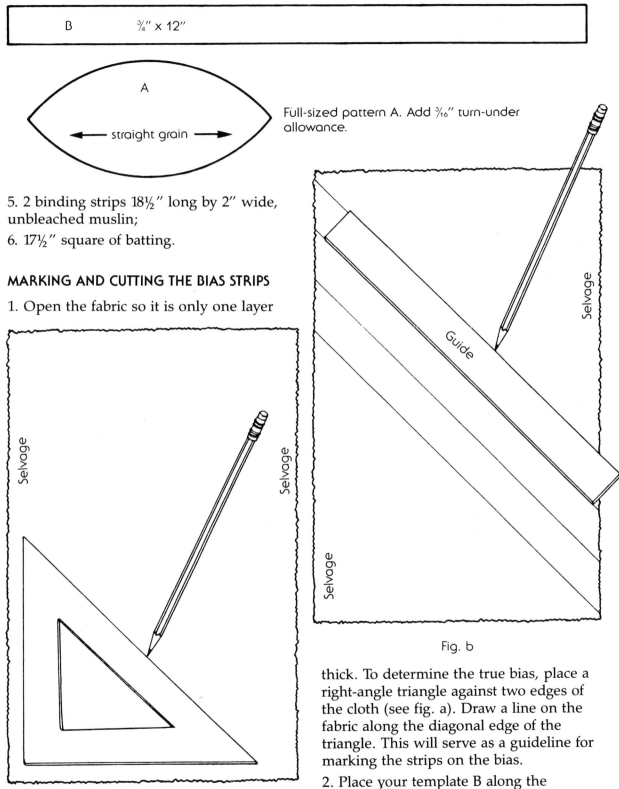

A

straight grain

Full-sized pattern A. Add ³⁄₁₆" turn-under allowance.

5. 2 binding strips 18½" long by 2" wide, unbleached muslin;

6. 17½" square of batting.

MARKING AND CUTTING THE BIAS STRIPS

1. Open the fabric so it is only one layer

Selvage

Selvage

Selvage

Selvage

Guide

Fig. b

thick. To determine the true bias, place a right-angle triangle against two edges of the cloth (see fig. a). Draw a line on the fabric along the diagonal edge of the triangle. This will serve as a guideline for marking the strips on the bias.

2. Place your template B along the

Fig. a

guideline and mark several strips (about four) across the fabric (see fig. b).*Do not* allow for turn-under allowances between the strips—this has already been *included* in the width of template B. Cut the strips apart.

PIECING ORDER

The Wreath is done entirely in appliqué. First a circle made from bias strips is appliquéd onto the background. Then the leaves are added at prescribed intervals around the outer and inner edges of the circle.

PINNING AND STITCHING

Refer to the appliqué instructions on page 47-50.

1. Prepare all the A pieces for appliqué. First, carefully clip the curved edges just to the marked lines. *Do not* clip the points (see fig. c). Turn under a triangular bit of fabric at the very tip of each end of the leaf

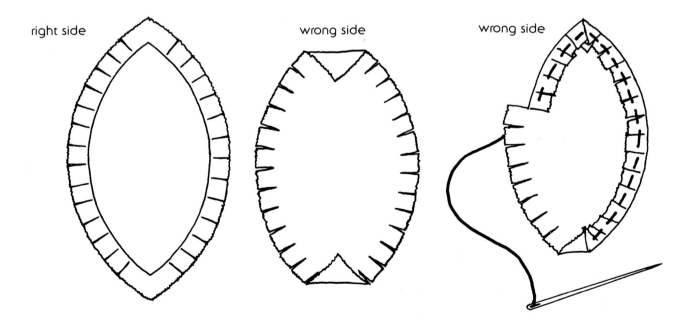

right side   wrong side   wrong side

Fig. c   Fig. d   Fig. e

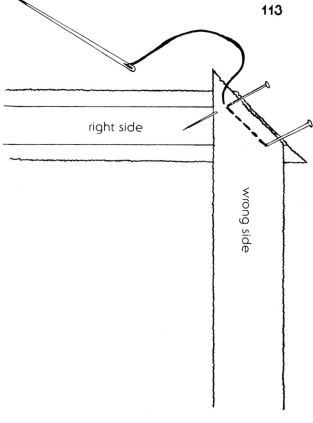

(see fig. d). Then fold down the curved edges, exactly on the marked lines (see fig. e). Finger press. Carefully trim any extra bulk at the points. Baste.

2. Working on the right side of each bias strip, measure and mark ¼" away from both long edges. A quilter's quarter works very well for this task. To join the strips into one continous length, place two strips together, right sides facing, at right angles to each other (see fig. f). The end points of each strip will not match exactly, but will be slightly offset. Pin and stitch together using a ¼" seam. Press the seam *open*. Trim away the excess points evenly. Continue joining strips in this manner until the entire piece measures about 36".

3. Prepare the long bias strip for appliqué. Fold under one long edge just on the marked line. Press lightly with an iron. Fold under the remaining side so that the raw edge doesn't quite meet the first fold. *Finger press.* Run a line of basting stitches down the center of the strip. The strip should measure approximately ¼" to ⅜" wide.

4. To mark the background block for appliqué placement, first fold the 16½" square into four square sections. Press the folds to crease. Open the fabric out; then fold again, but along one diagonal to form a large triangle. Press to crease, taking care not to remove the previous creases. Repeat this step with the second diagonal. The creases should appear exactly as they do in fig. g. To mark the circular placement line, place the point of the compass at the very center of the background where all the creases intersect. Set the radius for 5" and lightly draw a circle onto the fabric. The diameter of the completed circle should measure 10". If a compass is not available, a 10" diameter dinner plate or bowl can serve as a "template."

Fig. f

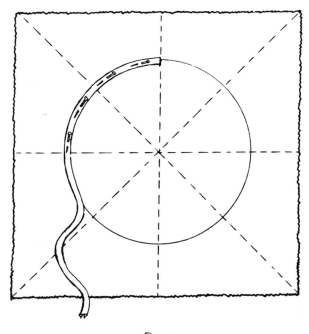

Fig. g

5. Starting at any point on the circle, center the prepared bias strip over the placement line. Pin the strip into place carefully without causing the background fabric to bunch up (see fig. g). End the strip exactly where you began, overlapping the beginning by about ½". Cut off any leftover bias strip. For a neat ending, fold under the edge of the overlapping bias strip a bit, about ¼". Make certain that the raw edges are hidden under the bias strip. Baste the strip into place, removing the pins as you go.

6. Appliqué the bias strip to the background first along the entire inner edge, then along the outer edge. Remember to match the thread to the bias strip. Carefully remove the basting stitches when the appliqué process is completed.

7. Pin and baste eight prepared leaves around the *outer* edge of the circle on the eight crease lines (see appliqué diagram). The bottom points of the leaves should just touch the edge of the bias strip, not overlap it. Tilt the leaves slightly to the left to create a sense of motion. Pin and baste eight more leaves to the outer edge, placing each one halfway between the first set of leaves. Pin and baste the remaining eight leaves around the *inner* edge of the circle on the eight crease lines.

8. Appliqué each leaf to the background, matching the thread to each fabric. Remove the basting stitches.

9. Steam iron the completed Wreath, carefully removing the creases in the background and pressing the leaves and circle flat.

QUILTING

1. Using the template for piece A, mark a very simple four-leafed motif in the center of the Wreath (see quilting diagram a). Or, if you prefer, trace the full-sized flower motif also illustrated (quilting diagram b). Transfer it to the center using the dressmaker's carbon method described on pg. 68. The remainder of the Wreath is outline-quilted which, in this instance, needs no marking.

Appliqué diagram

Quilting diagram a

2. Sandwich and baste the backing, batting, and appliqué top together (see pg. 14).

3. Quilt the center motif first. Then outline-quilt each leaf and both sides of the bias strip circle very close to the appliqué's edges, about ⅛" to ⅟₁₆" away (see quilting diagram again).

FINISHING

1. Remove the basting stitches.

2. Trim the excess batting and backing evenly with the appliquéd top.

3. Pin and stitch the two 17½"-long binding strips to parallel edges on the quilted block.

4. Repeat step 3 with the two 18½"-long binding strips on the remaining edges.

Quilting diagram b

18. Hearts: A Quilter's Valentine

As the traditional symbol of love, hearts have often been stitched into many marriage and friendship quilts, either in the quilting design or as appliqués. The Heart pattern presented here almost overflows with appliquéd and quilted hearts. What an opportunity for you to create a very special valentine!

When selecting fabrics, you will probably want to work with the color most often associated with hearts—red. All the appliqués can be made from the same fabric; however, if this seems too easy or too ordinary, try combining several red prints and/or solids to add a little more variety. Sometimes pink or purple hearts can be worked in successfully if you would like to break away from an all-red color scheme. A printed as well as a solid background can be especially effective in emphasizing solid-colored hearts. As always, though, choose colors and fabrics which best express your own creativity.

TOOLS

Assemble the template and sewing supplies listed on pgs. 10-12.

FABRIC REQUIREMENTS

A 21" (completed size) Heart block requires:

1. ⅜ yard 45"-wide pre-washed solid-red cotton fabric or scraps of various red prints;
2. ¾ yard of 45"-wide pre-washed cotton fabric for background, coordinating print or solid;
3. ¾ yard of 45"-wide pre-washed unbleached muslin for backing;
4. ¼ yard of 45"-wide pre-washed cotton fabric for binding, any coordinating color;
5. Polyester batting.

TEMPLATES

Prepare one template each for pieces A through D from the full-sized pattern pieces. Refer to the instructions on pgs. 12-13.

MARKING AND CUTTING THE FABRIC

Mark and cut pieces A through D according to the directions for appliqué (see pg. 46). The remaining pieces are marked and cut in the usual manner. The Heart block requires:

1. 1 A piece, solid red;
2. 2 B pieces, solid red;
3. 2 C pieces, solid red;
4. 2 D pieces, solid red;

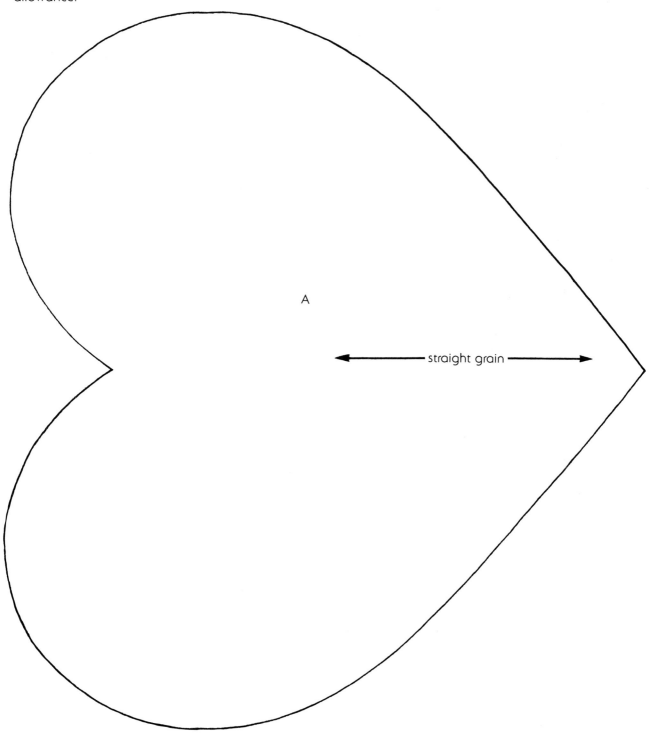

Full-sized pattern piece. Add ³⁄₁₆" turn-under allowance.

A

◄──────── straight grain ────────►

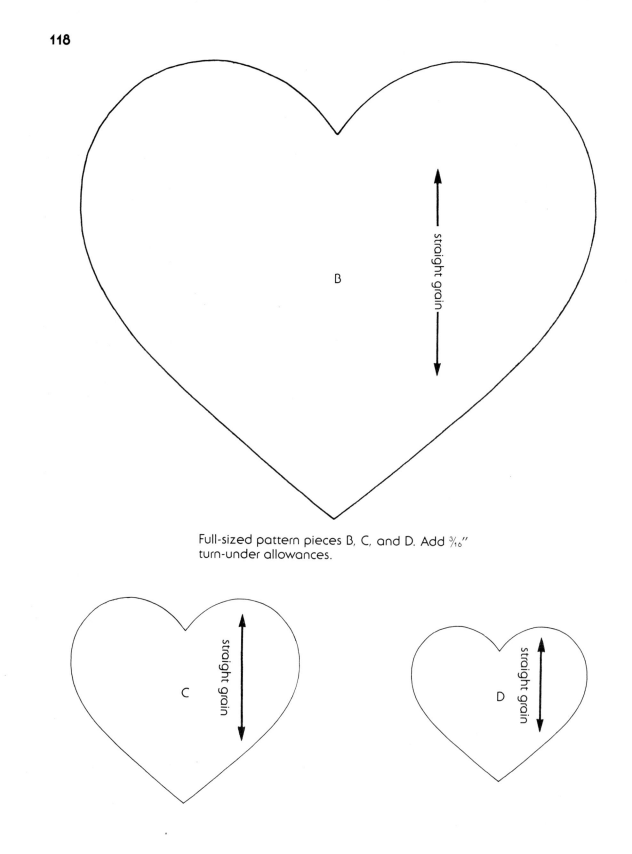

Full-sized pattern pieces B, C, and D. Add ³⁄₁₆″ turn-under allowances.

1. Prepare each heart piece for appliqué. First, carefully clip the deep inward curve with one straight cut, practically touching the marked line. Then make one diagonal cut on either side of it. Clip the remainder of the turn-under allowances at frequent intervals, especially around the sharp curves (see fig. a). Begin folding and basting the allowances under at the point

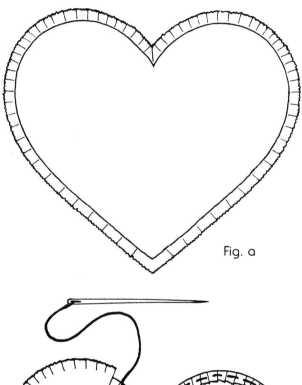

Fig. a

Fig. b

5. 21½ " square for background, print or solid fabric;

6. 22½ " square for backing, unbleached muslin;

7. 2 binding strips 22½ " long by 2" wide, any coordinating fabric;

8. 2 binding strips 23½ " long by 2" wide, any coordinating fabric;

9. 22½ " square of batting.

PIECING ORDER

Each heart is appliquéd onto the background in an easy-to-follow arrangement. Refer to the appliqué diagram to help place the hearts onto the background correctly.

PINNING AND STITCHING

Only simple appliqué techniques are required to construct the Heart block. Refer to the instructions on pgs. 47-50.

on the bottom, as was done in chapter 17 (Wreath). When you reach the deep inward curve, fold the allowances to the side of the straight cut. Run one basting stitch into the appliqué itself to help anchor the allowances down (see fig. b). Proceed around the other side of the inward curve and finish folding and basting the remaining edge.

2. To mark the appliqué placement lines, fold the 21½" background square into four square sections. Press the folds to crease. Open the fabric out, fold along one diagonal, and press to crease. Repeat this step with the second diagonal. The creases should appear as they do in the appliqué diagram.

each above and below the center heart; one D each to the right and left of the heart.

4. Appliqué the hearts to the background, beginning with the center and working outward. Match the thread color to the appliqués. Remove the basting stitches as you complete the appliqué process.

5. Press the completed top to remove the creases in the background and to flatten the appliqués a bit.

QUILTING

1. Mark the quilting lines as shown in the quilting diagram, about ½" away from the edges of each heart.

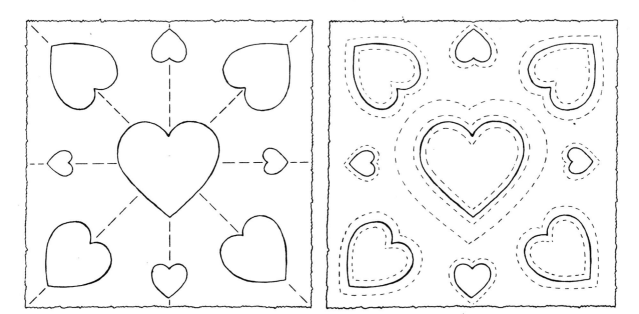

Appliqué diagram   Quilting diagram

3. Pin and baste the prepared appliqués to the background, centering each over the appropriate crease as shown in the appliqué diagram. Place A in the center; one B in each corner, pointing outward; one C

2. Sandwich and baste the backing, batting, and appliqué top together (see pgs. 14-15).

3. Quilt along the marked lines.

FINISHING

1. Remove the basting stitches.

2. Trim the excess batting and backing evenly with the quilted top.

3. Pin and stitch the two 22½"-long binding strips to parallel edges (see pg. 31).

4. Repeat step 3 with the 23½"-long binding strips on the remaining edges.

19. Tulips: A Spring Garden of Appliqué Flowers

WHEN THE TULIPS are in bloom, spring most assuredly has arrived. And even though their bright, cheerful colors fade all too soon, some of their beauty remains behind, captured by the skill and artistry of the quilter's needle. What warmth and comfort a Tulip quilt would provide on even the coldest winter night.

Select vivid spring colors—either solid or printed—for this pattern. Each tulip can be of a different color or simply shades of one color. For your inspiration, recall your images of spring and try to capture that feeling in fabric.

TOOLS

Assemble the template and sewing supplies listed on pgs. 10-12.

FABRIC REQUIREMENTS

A 16" (completed size) Tulip block requires:

1. Scraps or less than ¼ yard each of 45"-wide pre-washed cotton fabric, colors #1, #2, and #3;

2. ¼ yard of 45"-wide pre-washed cotton fabric, green;

3. ¾ yard of 45"-wide pre-washed cotton fabric for background, backing, and binding, solid white;

4. Polyester batting.

TEMPLATES

Prepare one template each for pieces A and B, using the full-sized pattern pieces. Refer to the instructions on pgs. 12-13.

Prepare a guide for piece C bias strip, just as you would a template, using the measurements provided.

MARKING AND CUTTING THE FABRIC

Mark and cut pieces A and B, following the instructions for appliqué (see pg. 46). For the B piece, cut one as per usual. Then reverse the template to mark the second piece needed. This will allow both leaves to turn in toward the stem when they are appliquéd. Mark and cut piece C according to the bias strip directions on pgs. 111-12. The Tulip block requires:

1. 1 A piece of each color #1 through #3;

2. 2 B pieces, green;

3. 28" total length of bias strip C, green;

4. 16½" square for background, white;

5. 17½" square for backing, white;

6. 2 binding strips 17½" long by 2" wide, white;

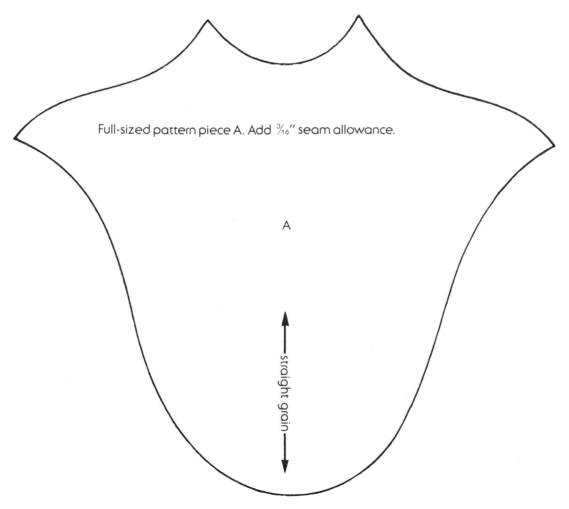

Full-sized pattern piece A. Add ³⁄₁₆″ seam allowance.

A

straight grain

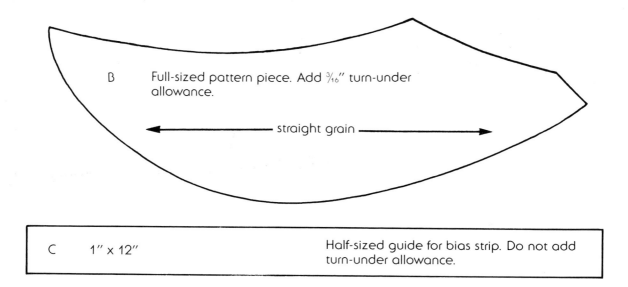

B   Full-sized pattern piece. Add ³⁄₁₆″ turn-under allowance.

←——————— straight grain ———————→

C   1″ x 12″   Half-sized guide for bias strip. Do not add turn-under allowance.

7. 2 binding strips 18½″ long by 2″ wide, white;

8. 17½″ square of batting.

PIECING ORDER

The tulips are arranged quite simply on the background fabric. Once the long stem and one tulip are situated properly, the remaining stems, tulips, and leaves can be placed more casually into position. For this pattern, there is no strict position for each piece. Slight variations will be more interesting and more naturalistic. Refer to the appliqué and quilting diagrams for assistance in positioning the appliqués onto the background.

PINNING AND STITCHING

To construct the Tulip block, follow the appliqué instructions on pgs. 47-50.

1. Prepare the tulips and leaves for appliqué. Be certain to follow the clipping steps explained in Chapter 18 for sharp and deep curves.

2. Join the bias strips together into one continuous length (see pg. 113). Prepare the edges of the bias strip for appliqué. Its final width should measure approximately ½″.

3. Fold the 16½″ background square in half along the right-hand diagonal. Press the fold to crease.

4. Beginning at the lower left-hand corner of the background, center the bias strip over the diagonal crease. End the strip about 7½″ from the upper right-hand corner (see fig. a). Pin, then baste into place.

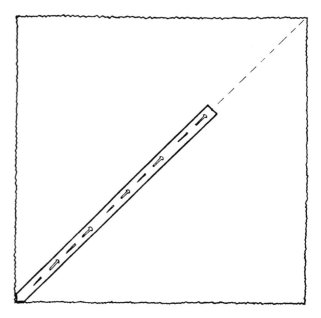

Fig. a

Place a 3½″ length of bias strip to the right of the main stem, about 5″ down from the top. Curve the smaller stem slightly. Tuck the end of this stem under the main stem by about ¼″. Pin, then baste into place (see fig. b).

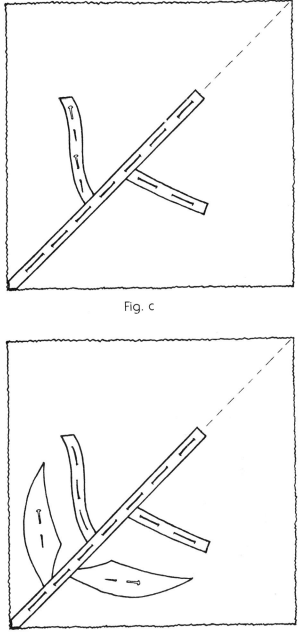

Fig. c

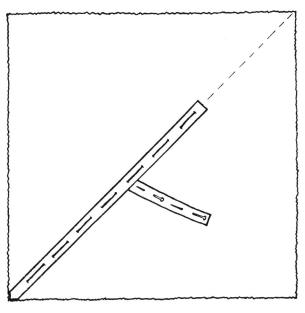

Fig. b

Place a 5½″ length of bias strip to the left of the main stem, about 7″ down from the top. Curve the stem and tuck the end under as before (see fig. c). Pin and baste into place.

5. Pin and baste the leaves to either side of the base of the main stem, tucking the ends under the stem (see fig. d). Before appliquéing the stems and leaves, place one tulip on the end of each stem to be certain all the pieces fit nicely onto the background. Now is the time to make any necessary adjustments. Remove the tulips.

6. Appliqué both sides of all stems and leaves to the background, matching the thread color to the stems and leaves. Make certain to stitch through *all thicknesses* where the leaves and smaller stems are tucked under the main stem.

Fig. d

7. Pin and baste one tulip to the end of each stem, overlapping it by about ¼″. Appliqué to the background with a color thread to match each tulip. Again, be certain to stitch through all thicknesses at the overlapping areas.

8. Remove all the basting stitches.

9. Press the completed Tulip block.

QUILTING

1. To mark the quilting lines for the center of the leaves and tulips, refer to the quilting diagram. These lines can be drawn freehand following the curves of the appliqués. The remainder of the block is outline-quilted very closely, so no marking is necessary.

2. Sandwich and baste the backing, batting, and appliqué top together (see pgs. 14-15).

3. Quilt along the marked lines. Then, outline quilt around each tulip, leaf, and stem, about ⅛" away from the edges of the appliqués. Outline quilt *inside* each tulip as well (see quilting diagram again.)

FINISHING

1. Remove the basting stitches.

2. Trim the excess batting and backing evenly with the quilted top.

3. Pin and stitch the two 17½"-long binding strips to parallel edges (see pg. 31).

4. Repeat step 3 with the two 18½"-long binding strips on the remaining edges.

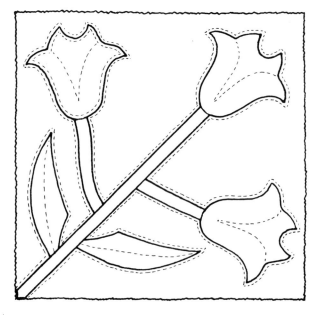

Quilting diagram

20. Sunflower: A Summer's Delight

PROUDLY AND CHEERFULLY, the Sunflower will display your appliqué skills. And perhaps the sense of accomplishment gained here will urge you to try more complicated appliqué designs as your quiltmaking career continues.

Because the design is so realistic, selecting colors for the Sunflower will present little difficulty. Draw on your talents for combining prints and solids to create subtle variations between the different pieces.

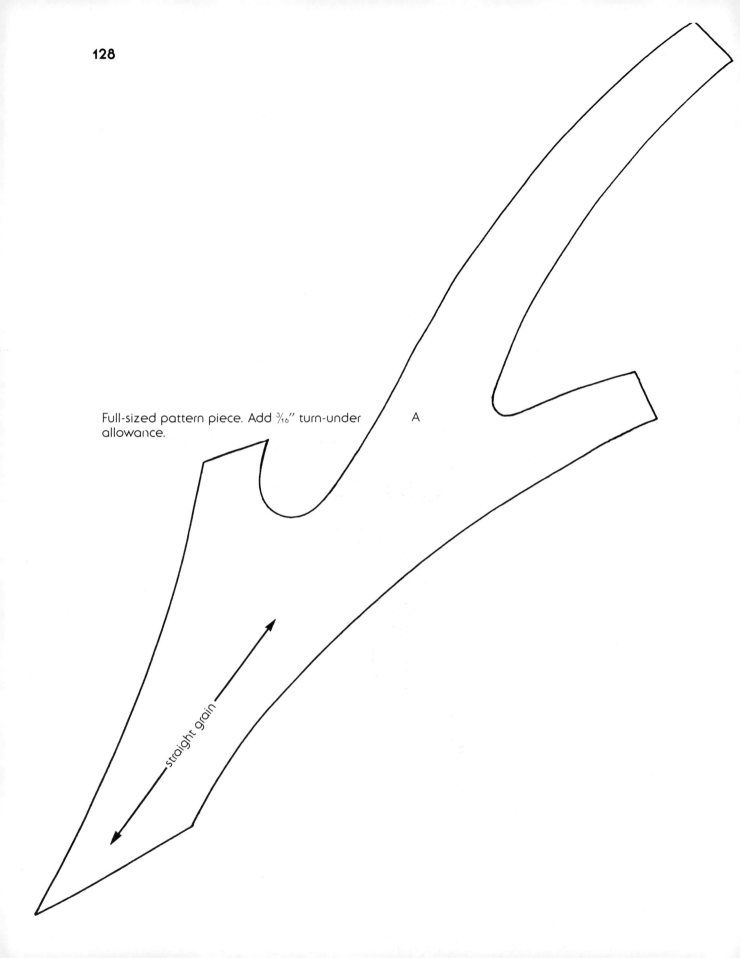

Full-sized pattern piece. Add ³⁄₁₆″ turn-under allowance.

A

straight grain

TOOLS

Assemble the template and sewing supplies listed on pgs. 10-12.

FABRIC REQUIREMENTS

A 12″ by 22″ (completed size) Sunflower block requires:

1. ¼ yard each of 45″-wide pre-washed cotton fabric; yellow, brown, and green;

2. ⅞ yard of 45″-wide pre-washed unbleached muslin for background and backing;

3. Polyester batting.

TEMPLATES

Prepare one template each for pieces A through E from the full-sized patterns. Refer to the instructions on pgs. 12-13.

MARKING AND CUTTING THE FABRIC

Mark and cut the fabric according to the instructions for appliqué (see pg. 46). The Sunflower block requires:

1. 1 A piece, green;

2. 1 B piece, green;

3. 1 C piece, green;

4. 13 D pieces, yellow;

5. 1 E piece, brown;

6. 12½″ by 22½″ rectangle for background, unbleached muslin;

7. 13½″ by 23½″ rectangle for backing, unbleached muslin;

8. 2 binding strips 13½″ long by 2″ wide, brown;

9. 2 binding strips 24½″ long by 2″ wide, brown;

10. 13½″ by 23½″ rectangle of batting.

PIECING ORDER

The stem, leaves, and flower are appliquéd onto the background fabric in several steps, overlapping the pieces to create a sense of dimension.

B

Full-sized pattern B. Add ³⁄₁₆″ turn-under allowance.

straight grain

Full-sized pattern pieces C, D, and E. Add ³⁄₁₆"
turn-under allowances.

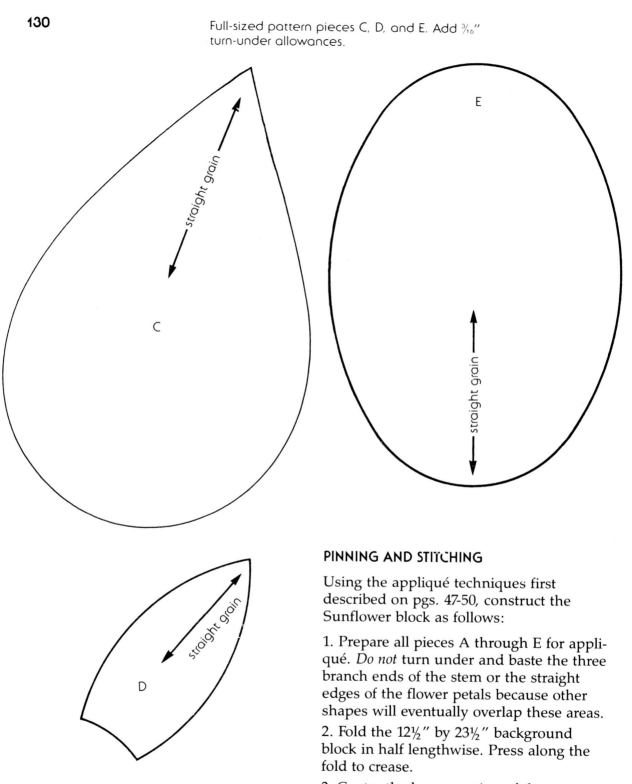

PINNING AND STITCHING

Using the appliqué techniques first
described on pgs. 47-50, construct the
Sunflower block as follows:

1. Prepare all pieces A through E for appliqué. *Do not* turn under and baste the three
branch ends of the stem or the straight
edges of the flower petals because other
shapes will eventually overlap these areas.

2. Fold the 12½" by 23½" background
block in half lengthwise. Press along the
fold to crease.

3. Center the lower portion of the stem
(piece A) over the crease with the pointed

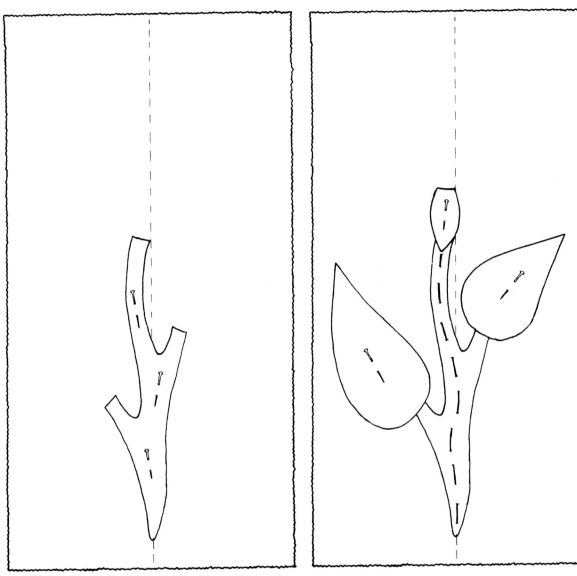

Fig. a

Fig. b

end about 1½″ from the bottom edge of the background fabric (see fig. a). Pin and baste into place. Then appliqué to the background.

4. Pin and baste piece C to the left-hand branch of the stem, overlapping the end by about ¼″. Repeat with piece B on the right-hand branch (see fig. b). Then appliqué each leaf onto the background, stitching through *all* thicknesses where the pieces overlap.

5. Pin one piece D to the top of piece A, overlapping the seam by about ½″ (see fig. b). Place the template for piece E on the background so that it overlaps the straight edge of piece D by ¼″. Draw around the template (see fig. c). This will serve as a guideline for positioning the remaining D pieces.

6. Arrange the petals (piece D) around the guideline, spacing them as evenly as possible. The straight edge of each petal should

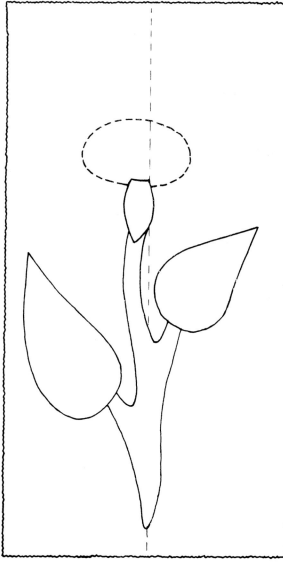

Fig. c

Fig. d

be about ¼″ *inside* the guideline. Pin and baste into place (see fig. d). Then appliqué only the prepared edges of the petals to the background.

7. Center piece E over the petals; pin and baste. Finally, appliqué piece E to the background, again stitching through all thicknesses.

8. Carefully remove all basting stitches.

9. Press the completed Sunflower block.

QUILTING

1. Sandwich and baste the backing, batting, and appliqué top together (see pgs. 14-15).

2. Outline-quilt around the entire Sunflower, about ⅛″ away from the edges of the appliqués.

Quilting diagram

FINISHING

1. Remove the basting stitches.

2. Trim the excess batting and backing evenly with the quilted top.

3. Pin and stitch the two 13½"-long binding strips to the shorter ends of the block (see pg. 31).

4. Repeat step 3 with the two 24½"-long binding strips on the remaining edges.

Appendix: Assembling A Bed-Size Quilt

EVEN THOUGH each chapter of this book deals with the construction, quilting, and finishing of a single block, many of the patterns can be used to make a bed-size quilt. The beginner would be wise to start small—perhaps with a crib or twin-size quilt. Smaller projects are less overwhelming in the amounts of time and effort required for successful completion.

After selecting the pattern, the next step is to determine the finished dimensions of the quilt. Measure the sleeping area of the quilt. Usually, it is this area which is covered by the pattern blocks. Then, determine how many blocks are needed to cover the width of the bed by dividing it by the *finished* size of a single pattern block. If the answer contains a fraction, round it off to the closest whole number. Figure the number of blocks required to cover the length of the bed in the same manner.

For example: The Churn Dash (12″ completed size) has been chosen to make a quilt for a twin-size bed (39″ wide by 75″ long). Divide the width of the bed by 12″ for an answer of 3.25. Rounded off, a minimum of three Churn Dash blocks is required to cover the width of the bed. Then divide the length by 12″ for an answer of 6.25. Rounded off, a minimum of six blocks is needed to cover the length of the bed.

A quilt, however, seldom covers just the sleeping area of a bed. Instead, it should be large enough so that the edges drape over the sides of the bed, covering the thickness of the mattress (about 7″). Therefore, the patchwork section must somehow be made larger. One solution is to increase the number of pattern blocks, either lengthwise, widthwise, or both. Or, adding plain border strips to each side of the patchwork will not only enlarge it, but will also frame the patterned top. Often, a combination of both methods is used.

For example: a twin-size Churn Dash quilt with borders can be made in two ways. First, increase the width by one block so that the patchwork section is four blocks wide by six blocks long, or 48″ by 72″. Then, 7″-wide borders are added to each side for a total measurement of 62″ by 86″. For a quilt with smaller borders, increase the total number of pattern blocks so that the patchwork section is five blocks wide by seven blocks long, or 60″ by 84″. Add 2″-wide borders to each side for a total measurement of 64″ by 88 ″.

It is also possible to make a quilt without any borders, giving the quilt a quaint, primitive appearance. Use the same formula described above to figure how many blocks are needed to cover the sleeping area plus the thickness of the mattress on all four sides. When the border strips are eliminated, however, it may be more difficult to achieve final dimensions that are close enough to the actual measurements needed to cover the bed adequately. Depending on the size of the pattern block, the result may be a quilt somewhat smaller or larger than required. For example: if the Churn Dash top is five blocks wide by seven blocks long, it will measure 60″ by 84″ and will cover a twin-size bed nicely, even without borders. If fewer blocks are used in both the width and length, the result would be a quilt that would cover only the sleeping area.

It is easy to see why careful planning, measuring, and figuring are important. Sketch several drawings of the proposed quilt on graph paper. Show all the variations possible with different numbers of pattern blocks and border widths. This will not only ensure that the quilt will be properly sized, but it will also help you visualize the finished effect. Think of yourself as a quilt architect—rearrange and redesign the quilt top as necessary until it has a pleasing, well-balanced overall appearance.

While making sketches, you will also need to decide on how the pattern blocks will be "set together." A solid set joins one pattern block to another, row after row, giving the quilt a very colorful, energetic look. A solid set requires a great deal of patchwork and affords less opportunity for fancy quilting. Sometimes in a solid set quilt, unexpected—but visually exciting—secondary patterns will emerge. For a quieter, more refined appearance, the pattern blocks can be alternated in checkerboard fashion with plain squares of equal size. A quilt in this style requires less patchwork but more quilting. The plain squares can be filled with simple straight line designs or with flower, feather, or wreath motifs. Each set has its own advantages, but with quite different effects. Sketch the proposed quilt both ways, then decide which style best enhances the pattern and expresses your own creativity.

After the overall dimensions and the set have been established, it is time to figure just how many patches of each shape and color must be cut. The marking and cutting section of each chapter has already determined how many pieces are needed for a single block. All you need to do is multiply each of these by the total number of blocks required to construct the whole quilt. For example: if four A pieces are needed for one block, forty A pieces are needed for ten blocks. As you figure, keep a chart showing the totals.

Perhaps the least exciting aspect of quiltmaking is figuring the yardage requirements for the patches, borders, and backing. As previously stated, the fabric requirements given in each chapter are overestimated. Therefore, if you multiply the figure given by the total number of blocks to be constructed, you will actually have more fabric than is really necessary. Of course, you may figure the yardage this way and save the extra fabric for future projects.

Some simple arithmetic will help calculate the yardage requirements more economically. First, determine how many pieces of one particular shape will fit across the width of the material. Even though most fabrics suitable for quilting are 45″ wide, the actual useable width is only about 42″. Shrinkage and trimming the selvages account for the loss of three inches. Now, suppose that a total of forty 4″-square patches is needed for a quilt top. Each pattern piece must first be adjusted to include the seam allowances, so the 4″ square will actually be a 4½″ square. Divide 42″ (the useable width of the fabric) by 4.5 (the size of the pattern piece) for an answer of nine (rounded off). Therefore, nine 4½″ squares will fit across the width of the material.

Next, calculate how many rows are needed by dividing the total number of patches (forty) by the number of pieces per row (nine). The answer is 4.4, rounded off to 5. (In calculating the number of rows, round off to the *higher* number.)

Finally, determine the length of fabric needed to accommodate one row. In this example, 4½″ are required. Multiply this length by the number of rows (five) for an answer of 22½″ or ⅝ yard. Allowing a little extra for cutting errors and shrinkage, the total fabric requirement is ¾ yard.

Repeat these calculations for all pattern pieces, borders, plain squares, and binding strips. Total the amounts of like fabrics into yards to reach the final requirements.

The backing fabric for many small quilts can be obtained from one width of material. In this instance, only the length in yards needs to be figured. The backing for any quilt wider than 42″, however, must be pieced. For example: if a quilt top measures 62″ by 86″, one piece of fabric 42″ wide, seamed to another one 21″ wide (each 87″ or 2½ yards long), will provide an adequate backing. The total fabric requirement will be 5 yards.

There is no need to figure the yardage requirements for the batting. Packaged rolls of batting already cut to various quilt sizes are available in fabric and quilt shops. Purchase one whose measurements are closest to those of the quilt top.

The remaining steps for constructing a bed-size quilt simply repeat those for making a single-pattern block. Marking, cutting, pinning, and stitching the patches are described fully in each chapter.

After the patchwork blocks have been completed, they are joined into horizontal rows according to the sketch made during the planning stage. Then the rows are joined to one another. Pin and stitch the patchwork and plain blocks together in exactly the same way that the small pattern squares are joined in the Nine-Patch chapter.

Then add two border strips to the longer sides of the patchwork section. Their width was determined when the quilt was first planned, and their length must equal the overall length of the patchwork plus the usual ¼″ seam allowances. Finally, add the border strips to the shorter sides. They should be the same width as the others and long enough to cover the overall width of the patchwork plus the first set of borders.

Quilting, sandwiching and basting the layers together, and finishing a bed-size quilt are essentially the same as for the individual blocks, except that you will be working on a larger scale. These steps are described fully in each chapter.

However, no suggestions are given for quilting designs to fill the border strips or alternating plain squares. Straight lines, diamonds, or other simple geometric shapes are easy and attractive quilting motifs. Many books containing fancier designs such as cables, flowers, or feathers are available in quilt and book shops. Select quilting designs according to your ability. Start with simple motifs, then graduate to more difficult ones as your quilting skills improve.

Suggested Reading

Bacon, Lenice Ingram. *American Patchwork Quilts.* New York: William Morrow, 1973.

Bannister, Barbara. *The United States Pattern Patchwork Book.* New York: Dover Publications, Inc., 1976.

Beyer, Alice. *Quilting.* Reprint of 1934 edition. Albany, Ca.: East Bay Heritage Quilters, 1978.

Beyer, Jinny. *Patchwork Patterns.* McLean, Va.: EPM Publications, Inc., 1979.

_____. *The Quilter's Album of Blocks and Borders.* McLean, Va.: EPM Publications, Inc., 1980.

Bishop, Robert. *Quilts, Coverlets, Rugs & Samplers.* New York: Alfred A. Knopf, 1982.

Bishop, Robert, and Patricia Coblentz. *New Discoveries in American Quilts.* New York: E.P. Dutton, Inc., 1976.

Bishop, Robert, and Elizabeth Safanda. *A Gallery of Amish Quilts: Design and Diversity from a Plain People.* New York: E.P. Dutton, Inc., 1976.

Brightbill, Dorothy. *Quilting as a Hobby.* New York: Sterling Publishing Co., 1963.

Carroll, Amy, ed. *Patchwork and Appliqué.* New York: Ballantine Books, 1981.

Chase, Patti, and Mimi Dolbier. *The Contemporary Quilt: New American Quilts and Fabric Art.* New York: E.P. Dutton, Inc., 1978.

Colby, Averil. *Patchwork.* Watertown, Mass.: Charles T. Branford Co., 1958.

_____. *Patchwork Quilts.* New York: Charles Scribner's Sons, 1966.

_____. *Quilting.* New York: Charles Scribner's Sons, 1971.

Cooper, Patricia, and Norma B. Buferd. *Quilters: Women and Domestic Arts.* New York: Doubleday & Co., Inc., 1978.

Echols, Margit. *The New American Quilt.* New York: Doubleday & Co., Inc., 1976.

Finley, Ruth E. *Old Patchwork Quilts and the Women Who Made Them.* Watertown, Mass.: Charles T. Branford Co., 1971.

Fisher, Katharine. *Quilting in Squares.* New York: Charles Scribner's Sons, 1978.

Fitzrandolph, Mavis, and Florence M. Fletcher. *Quilting.* Woodbridge, N.J.: The Dryad Press, 1972.

Fox, Sandi. *Small Endearments: 19th-Century Quilts for Children.* New York: Charles Scribner's Sons, 1984.

Gammell, Alice I. *Polly Prindles' Book of American Patchwork Quilts.* New York: Grosset & Dunlap, Inc., 1973.

Gutcheon, Beth. *The Perfect Patchwork Primer.* New York: David McKay Co., Inc., 1973.

Gutcheon, Beth and Jeffrey. *The Quilt Design Workbook.* New York: Rawson Associates Publishers, Inc., 1976.

Haas, Louis Krause, and Robert Bartlett. *Quilts, Counterpanes and Related Fabrics.* Santa Monica, Ca.: Coromandel House, 1956.

Haders, Phyllis. *The Main Street Pocket Guide to Quilts.* Pittstown, N.J.: The Main Street Press, 1983.
_____. *Sunshine and Shadow: The Amish and Their Quilts.* Pittstown, N.J.: The Main Street Press, 1984.

Hall, Carrie A., and Rose Kretsinger. *The Romance of the Patchwork Quilt in America.* Reprint of 1935 edition. New York: Bonanza Books, n.d.

Hinson, Dolores A. *The Quilter's Companion.* New York: Arco Publishing Co., Inc., 1973.
_____. *Quilter's Manual.* New York: Hearthside Press, 1970.

Holstein, Jonathan. *Abstract Design in American Quilts.* New York: Whitney Museum of American Art, 1971.
_____. *The Pieced Quilt.* Greenwich, Conn.: New York Graphic Society, 1973.

Houck, Carter, and Myron Miller. *American Quilts and How to Make Them.* New York: Charles Scribner's Sons, 1975.

Ickis, Marguerite. *The Standard Book of Quilt Making and Collecting.* New York: Dover Publications Inc., 1949.

Ives, Suzy. *Patterns for Patchwork Quilts and Cushions.* Watertown, Mass.: Charles T. Branford, Co., 1977.

Johnson, Mary Elizabeth. *A Garden of Quilts.* Birmingham, Ala.: Oxmoor House, Inc., 1984.
_____. *Prize Country Quilts.* Birmingham, Ala.: Oxmoor House, Inc., 1977.

Khin, Yvonne. *The Collector's Dictionary of Quilt Names & Patterns.* Washington, D.C.: Acropolis Books, Ltd., 1980.

Kolter, Jane Bentley. *Forget Me Not: A Gallery of Friendship and Album Quilts.* Pittstown, N.J.: The Main Street Press, 1985.

LaBranche, Carol. *Patchwork Pictures.* Pittstown, N.J.: The Main Street Press, 1985.

Lewis, Alfred Allen. *The Mountain Artisan's Quilting Book.* New York: Macmillan & Co., 1973.

Lithgow, Marilyn. *Quiltmaking and Quiltmakers.* New York: Thomas Y. Crowell Co., 1974.

Mainardi, Patricia. *Quilts: The Great American Art.* San Pedro, Ca.: Miles and Weir, 1978.

Marston, Doris E. *Patchwork Today.* Watertown, Mass.: Charles T. Branford Co., 1968.

McCosh, Elizabeth. *Introduction to Patchwork.* New York: Taplinger, 1962.

McKim, Ruby. *One Hundred and One Patchwork Patterns.* New York: Dover Publications, Inc., 1962.

Newman, Thelma R. *Quilting, Patchwork, Appliqué and Trapunto: Traditional Methods and Original Designs.* New York: Crown Publishers, Inc., 1974.

Orlofsky, Patsy and Myron. *Quilts in America.* New York: McGraw-Hill Book Co., 1974.

Paddleford, Clementine. *Patchwork Quilts: A Collection of Forty-One Old Time Blocks.* New York: Farm and Fireside, n.d.

Pelletier, Henry Louis. *Favorite Patchwork Patterns: Full-Size Templates and Instructions for 12 Quilts.* New York: Dover Publications, 1984.

Roesler, John. *Rectangular Quilt Blocks.* Des Moines: Wallace-Homestead Book Co., 1983.

Safford, Carleton L., and Robert Bishop. *America's Quilts and Coverlets.* New York: E.P. Dutton, Inc., 1972.

Sommer, Elyse with Joellen Sommer. *A Patchwork, Appliqué and Quilting Primer.* New York: Lothrop, Lee & Shepard Co., 1975.

Timmins, Alice. *Patchwork Simplified.* New York: Arco Publishing Co., Inc., 1975.

Vogue Guide to Patchwork and Quilting. New York: Condé Nast, 1973.

Webster, Marie D. *Quilts—Their Story and How to Make Them.* Reprint of 1915 edition. New York: Tudor Publishing Co., 1948.

Wiebusch, Marguerite. *Feathers and Other Fancies.* Published by the author, 5400 W. 300 South, Russiaville, IN 46979, 1982.

Wilson, Erica. *Erica Wilson's Quilts of America.* Birmingham, Ala.: Oxmoor House, Inc., 1979.

Wiss, Audrey and Douglas. *Folk Quilts and How to Recreate Them.* Pittstown, N.J.: The Main Street Press, 1983.

Woodard, Thomas K., and Blanche Greenstein. *Crib Quilts and Other Small Wonders.* New York: E.P. Dutton, Inc., 1981.

Acknowledgments

THE AUTHOR'S original quilt block designs illustrated throughout this book have been inspired by many sources, among them the work of traditional quilters of several generations. Also shown in these pages are five full-size quilts. These are:

pg. 38, Checkerboard, 100% cotton, 46" x 56", made by the author, 1983;

pg. 78, Bow-Tie, 100% cotton, 84" x 96", made by the author, 1984;

pg. 87, Star, 100% cotton, 72" x 82", maker unknown, photograph courtesy of Susan Bilotte;

pg. 105, Wheel of Fortune, 100% cotton, 72" x 82", made by Florence Daquila, 1920, photograph courtesy of Ange Papparella;

pg. 123, Tulip, 100% cotton, 88" x 88", made by Pearl E. Flinner, 1968; photograph courtesy of Lois Feits.